Violet Harmond

HEART HEALTHY
Cookbook
FOR BEGINNERS

**1800 Days of Amazing Low-Sodium and Low-Fat Recipes
to Safeguard Your Heart Health.**

Includes a 60-Day Meal Plan + BONUS

Table of Content

Introduction

Something about me

My name is Violet Harmond and I was only eight years old when I found out I was diabetic. I still clearly remember the day my life changed forever. It was a hot summer day, and my family was celebrating my older brother's birthday. While everyone was enjoying the cake and sweets, I felt strangely weak and thirsty. Despite the many glasses of water I drank, the thirst never seemed to subside. My mother, worried about my state of health, decided to take me to hospital.

After a series of tests, I was diagnosed with type 1 diabetes. At that moment, I did not know exactly what it meant, but I saw my parents' worried faces and I knew something serious was happening. From that day on, my life changed dramatically. I had to learn to manage my condition, deal with insulin injections and carefully monitor my blood sugar levels.

I was not always able to manage my condition well and several times I found myself in danger. Diabetes has taken me through ups and downs, but it has also forged my character and determination. Facing this daily challenge has taught me to never take anything for granted and to take care of my body as if it were my most precious treasure.

Over the years, I decided to dedicate my life to supporting and helping people with diabetes. I specialised in diabetes care management and tried to share my knowledge through writing. After the publication of 'Type 2 diabetes cookbook for beginners' and 'DASH diet cookbook for beginners', I realised that there was still a lot to be done to provide useful and practical resources for those seeking to live a healthy life, not only for diabetics, but for anyone who wants to take care of their heart and their health in general.

Thus, my third book, 'Heart Healthy Cookbook for beginners', was born. This project was inspired by a young woman I met during one of my lectures. She had type 1 diabetes and was trying to adopt a healthy diet to improve her cardiovascular health. Her story touched me deeply, and I realised that there was an urgent need for a book that would provide delicious and nutritious recipes, suitable not only for diabetics, but for anyone wishing to follow a balanced diet for the heart.

This book is not just a collection of recipes, but a comprehensive guide to embracing a healthy lifestyle.

With a heart full of hope and determination, I invite you to embark with me on this journey towards a healthier and happier life. Whether you are diabetic, suffer from heart disease or simply wish to improve your health, I will accompany you on this journey to wellness. Be ready to discover new flavours, take care of your body and experience the joy of a healthy life full of vitality.

Happy journey to you all.

Violet Harmond.

Knowing about heart disease

Heart diseases, also known as cardiovascular diseases, represent a group of conditions involving the heart and blood vessels and are a major cause of morbidity and mortality worldwide. They can be of different types, but the most common include:

- **Coronary artery disease:** This is the most common form of heart disease and is caused by the formation of fatty and cholesterol plaques within the coronary arteries, which are responsible for supplying blood and oxygen to the heart. Plaques can restrict blood flow and cause angina (chest pain) or, in more severe cases, a heart attack (myocardial infarction).
- **Hypertension:** Also known as high blood pressure, hypertension is a condition in which the pressure of the blood against the walls of the arteries is constantly elevated. This can lead to an increased workload of the heart and increase the risk of cardiovascular disease, stroke and other complications.
- **Heart failure:** This is a condition in which the heart cannot pump enough blood to meet the body's needs. It can be caused by a variety of conditions, including coronary artery disease, hypertension, heart attack, valve disease and other conditions that impair heart function.
- **Heart valve disease:** Heart valves are structures that allow blood to flow in one direction through the heart. Valvular diseases can be caused by stenosis (narrowing) or insufficiency (regurgitation) of the valves and can lead to symptoms such as fatigue, breathlessness and swelling of the legs.
- **Cardiac arrhythmias:** These are disorders of the heart rhythm, which can involve heartbeats that are too fast, too slow or irregular. Some arrhythmias can be harmless, but others can be dangerous and require specific treatment.
- **Congenital heart diseases:** These are abnormalities present from birth that involve the structure of the heart or large blood vessels. They can be mild or severe and require surgery or other treatments.

Prevention and management of heart disease are of paramount importance. A healthy lifestyle, including a balanced diet, regular exercise, avoiding smoking and managing stress, can help reduce the risk of developing cardiovascular diseases. In addition, regular medical check-ups are essential, especially if you have risk factors such as diabetes, obesity, hypertension or a family history of heart disease.

Cause and symptoms of heart diseases

Heart disease can be caused by several factors, some of which are modifiable, while others are non-modifiable. The main causes of heart disease include:

Modifiable risk factors:

- **Unhealthy diet:** A high intake of saturated fat, cholesterol, salt and sugar can contribute to plaque build-up in the arteries.
- **Physical inactivity:** Lack of exercise can lead to an increased risk of heart disease.
- **Smoking:** Smoking damages blood vessels and increases the formation of plaque in the arteries.
- **High blood pressure (hypertension):** Constantly rising blood pressure damages the walls of the arteries and increases the risk of cardiovascular disease.
- **Obesity and overweight:** Excessive weight can contribute to the development of other conditions that increase the risk of heart disease, such as diabetes.
- **Diabetes:** The body's inability to adequately regulate blood sugar levels can damage blood vessels and the heart.

Non-modifiable risk factors:

- **Age:** The risk of heart disease increases with advancing age.
- **Gender:** Men have a higher risk than women, but women's risk increases after menopause.
- **Family history:** Having close relatives with a history of heart disease can increase the risk.

Symptoms of heart disease can vary depending on the type of condition and severity, but some common symptoms include:

- **Chest pain:** A feeling of tightness, burning or pain in the middle or left side of the chest, commonly known as angina. The pain may radiate to the left arm, neck, back or jaw.
- **Dyspnoea:** Difficulty breathing or shortness of breath, which may occur during physical activity or even at rest in severe cases.
- **Fatigue:** Fatigue and lack of energy even with little effort.
- **Palpitations:** Sensation of an accelerated, irregular or occasional heartbeat.
- **Leg swelling:** Retention of fluid that can cause swelling in the lower limbs.
- **Dizziness or fainting:** May occur when the heart is unable to pump sufficient blood to the brain.
- **Nausea or vomiting:** Symptoms that may occur in certain types of heart disease, especially in the presence of heart failure.
- **Excessive sweating:** Particularly cold sweating or excessive sweating during physical activity or in stressful situations.

Importantly, some individuals may be asymptomatic or have mild symptoms, so regular medical check-ups are essential, especially if you have risk factors or a family history of heart disease. Early diagnosis and appropriate management of risk factors can help prevent or delay the development of heart disease and improve quality of life.

How is heart disease treated

The treatment of heart disease depends on the type and severity of the condition. There are several treatment options available, which may include pharmacological interventions, invasive procedures and lifestyle modifications. Some of the main treatment approaches are listed below:

Medications: These are used to control symptoms, prevent complications and reduce the workload of the heart. Some common drugs used to treat heart disease include:

- **Beta-blockers:** They reduce heart rate and lower blood pressure.
- **ACE inhibitors or ARBs:** They help relax blood vessels and lower blood pressure.
- **Statins:** Reduce LDL-cholesterol and prevent plaque formation in the arteries.
- **Diuretics:** They help eliminate excess fluid from the body, thus reducing the burden on the heart.
- **Antiplatelet or anticoagulants:** They reduce the risk of blood clots and can be used in patients with coronary artery disease or atrial fibrillation.
- **Invasive procedures:** In some cases, surgery or an invasive procedure may be necessary to treat heart disease. Some examples include:
- **Coronary angioplasty:** Using an inflatable balloon, a partially or completely occluded coronary artery is opened, often followed by the insertion of a stent to keep the artery open.
- **Coronary bypass:** A new route for blood flow is created by bypassing the blocked coronary arteries.
- **Valvuloplasty:** A balloon is used to enlarge a stenotic heart valve and restore adequate blood flow.
- **Device implantation:** It may be necessary to implant pacemakers, defibrillators or other devices to help regulate heart rhythm or manage heart failure.

Lifestyle changes: This is an essential aspect of managing heart disease. People are encouraged to eat a healthy, balanced diet, adopt a regular exercise regime, stop smoking and manage stress. These changes can reduce risk factors and improve cardiovascular health.

Cardiac rehabilitation programmes: After a cardiac event or surgery, patients may be referred to cardiac rehabilitation programmes. These programmes include supervised exercises, instruction on risk factor management and emotional support.

Treatment of heart disease is always customised for each individual, taking into account risk factors, medical history and severity of the condition. Long-term management often requires a multidisciplinary approach, involving the cardiologist, family doctor and other specialists, as well as the active cooperation of the patient himself.

The 'Dietary Model for Heart Health'

Following the 'Dietary Model for Heart Health' is recommended because it can significantly help reduce the risk of heart disease and improve overall cardiovascular health. This dietary pattern is based on eating habits that have been extensively studied and proven beneficial for the heart. Here are some reasons why it is important to follow this type of dietary pattern:

- **Reduction of risk factors:** A heart-healthy diet can help reduce several risk factors for heart disease, such as LDL cholesterol ('bad cholesterol'), elevated blood pressure and inflammation.
- **Body weight control:** A balanced diet can help maintain a healthy body weight or achieve controlled weight loss, if necessary. Excess weight is associated with an increased risk of heart disease.
- **Reduction of inflammation:** Some foods in the heart-healthy eating pattern have anti-inflammatory properties, which can help reduce the risk of artery damage and promote heart health.
- **Support for vascular health:** This eating pattern is rich in nutrients that support healthy arteries and blood vessels, keeping them flexible and healthy.
- **Blood pressure control:** A heart-healthy diet rich in potassium, calcium and magnesium can help control blood pressure and reduce the risk of hypertension.
- **Improving cholesterol levels:** A diet based on this model can help reduce LDL-cholesterol and increase HDL-cholesterol ('good cholesterol'), thus promoting heart health.
- **Blood glucose regulation:** A balanced diet based on whole foods and moderate levels of refined carbohydrates can help control blood glucose levels, reducing the risk of type 2 diabetes, a condition that may be associated with heart disease.

The heart-healthy eating pattern emphasises the consumption of fruit, vegetables, whole grains, lean sources of protein, healthy fats and limits the consumption of foods high in saturated fats, added sugars and salt. It combines elements of a Mediterranean diet, known for its cardiovascular benefits, and a DASH (Dietary Approaches to Stop Hypertension) diet. By adopting this dietary pattern, one can achieve numerous heart health benefits and improve long-term quality of life. However, it is important to consult with a health professional or dietician to tailor the diet to individual needs and specific health conditions.

Foods to eat and foods to avoid

In the dietary pattern for heart health, it is recommended to consume a variety of nutritious foods that support cardiovascular health. Some recommended foods and those to avoid are listed below:

Recommended foods for heart health:

- **Fruits:** Apples, pears, oranges, strawberries, blueberries, kiwis and other fresh fruits rich in vitamins, minerals and fibre.
- **Vegetables:** Spinach, broccoli, carrots, tomatoes, peppers, cauliflower, and other colourful vegetables, providing heart-healthy nutrients.
- **Whole grains:** Oats, barley, spelt, brown rice, wholemeal bread, wholemeal pasta and other whole-grain products, which are rich in fibre and nutrients.
- **Legumes:** Beans, lentils, chickpeas and peas, which are excellent sources of plant protein and fibre.
- **Nuts and seeds:** Walnuts, almonds, flax seeds, chia seeds and other seeds rich in healthy fats, protein and antioxidants.
- **Fish:** Salmon, mackerel, tuna, sardines and other fatty fish, rich in heart-healthy omega-3 fatty acids.
- **Vegetable oils:** Olive oil, linseed oil, canola oil, which contain heart-healthy monounsaturated and polyunsaturated fats.
- **Low-fat dairy products:** Skimmed milk, Greek yoghurt, low-fat cheeses, which provide calcium and protein without excess saturated fat.

Foods to avoid or limit:

- **Saturated fats:** Reduce consumption of fatty meat, butter, lard, bacon and high-fat dairy products.
- **Trans fats:** Avoid foods containing hydrogenated trans fats, such as snacks and packaged baked goods.
- **Salt:** Reduce excessive salt use and limit salty and processed foods.
- **Added sugars:** Reduce consumption of sweets, sugary drinks, concentrated fruit juices and foods high in added sugars.
- **Red meat:** Limit consumption of red meat and processed meats, such as sausages, cured meats and preserved meats.
- **Alcoholic beverages:** Consume in moderation, if at all, as excess alcohol can be harmful to the heart.

It is important to emphasise that the dietary pattern for heart health is based on a balanced and varied diet that provides a wide range of essential nutrients.

It is always advisable to consult with a health professional or nutritionist for personalised guidance tailored
to individual needs, also considering any pre-existing
medical conditions.

Recipes

There are many recipes in this cookbook. Many of
them are perfect for your heart's health, while others,
although designed for the same purpose, are to be
limited.

I am talking, for example, about red meat recipes. I
have included about 20 of them but I still advise you
to consume them sparingly, as well as dessert recipes.
I do not want to, and it is not fair to, completely eliminate all forms of forbidden food because good food
and healthy eating should not be your prison, but
common sense and moderation is equally important.

Breakfast

1. Veggie Egg Muffins

Preparation time: 15 minutes
Cook Time: 20 minutes
Servings: 6 muffins

Ingredients:

- 6 large eggs
- 1 cup fresh spinach, chopped
- 1/4 cup red bell pepper, diced
- 1/4 cup red onion, diced
- 1/4 cup cherry tomatoes, halved
- 1/4 tsp black pepper
- 1/4 tsp dried oregano
- Cooking spray

Instructions:

1. Preheat your oven to 350°F (175°C). Grease a 6-cup muffin tin with cooking spray or use silicone muffin liners for easy removal.
2. In a large mixing bowl, crack the eggs and whisk them until well beaten.
3. Add the chopped spinach, diced red bell pepper, red onion, and cherry tomatoes to the beaten eggs. Mix well to combine.
4. Sprinkle black pepper and dried oregano into the mixture and stir until evenly distributed.
5. Carefully pour the vegetable and egg mixture into each muffin cup, filling them about 3/4 full.
6. Place the muffin tin in the preheated oven and bake for approximately 18-20 minutes or until the egg muffins are set in the center.
7. Once done, remove the muffin tin from the oven and let the egg muffins cool for a few minutes.
8. Gently remove the egg muffins from the muffin tin or silicone liners.
9. Serve the Veggie Egg Muffins warm as a heart-healthy and low-fat breakfast or snack option.

Nutritional Information (per serving):
Cal: 70 | Carbs: 2g | Pro: 6g | Fat: 4g | Chol: 150mg | Sod: 65mg | Fiber: 1g | Sugars: 1g

2. Avocado Toast Delight

Preparation time: 5 minutes
Servings: 1

Ingredients:

- 1 ripe avocado
- 1 slice whole-grain bread
- 1 small tomato, sliced
- 1/4 tsp. lemon juice
- 1/8 tsp. garlic powder
- Pinch of salt (optional)
- Pinch of black pepper
- Fresh basil leaves, for garnish (optional)

Instructions:

1. Slice the ripe avocado in half, remove the pit, and scoop the flesh into a bowl.
2. Mash the avocado with a fork until it reaches your desired consistency.
3. Add lemon juice, garlic powder, a pinch of salt (if using), and black pepper to the mashed avocado. Mix well.
4. Toast the whole-grain bread until it reaches your desired level of crispiness.
5. Spread the mashed avocado mixture evenly on the toasted bread.
6. Top the avocado toast with sliced tomatoes.
7. Garnish with fresh basil leaves, if desired.
8. Serve immediately and enjoy your heart-healthy Avocado Toast Delight!

Nutritional Information (per serving):
Cal: 240 | Carbs: 21g | Pro: 4g | Fat: 17g | Chol: 0mg | Sod: 50mg | Fiber: 8g | Sugars: 3g

3. Chia Berry Parfait

Preparation time: 10 minutes
Servings: 2

Ingredients:

- 1 cup low-fat Greek yogurt
- 2 tbsp chia seeds
- 1 cup mixed berries (strawberries, blueberries, raspberries)
- 1 tsp honey (optional, for sweetness)
- 1/4 tsp vanilla extract (optional)

Instructions:

1. In a bowl, mix the low-fat Greek yogurt, chia seeds, and optional honey and vanilla extract. Stir well to combine.
2. In two serving glasses or small jars, start layering the parfait. Begin with a spoonful of the yogurt-chia mixture at the bottom.
3. Add a layer of mixed berries on top of the yogurt.
4. Repeat the layers until the glasses are filled, finishing with a layer of mixed berries on the top.
5. Cover the glasses with plastic wrap and refrigerate for at least 2 hours or overnight to allow the chia seeds to expand and thicken the mixture.
6. Before serving, you can add a few fresh berries on top for garnish.
7. Enjoy your heart-healthy Chia Berry Parfait!

Nutritional Information (per serving):
Cal: 150 | Carbs: 20g | Pro: 8g | Fat: 4g | Chol: 2mg | Sod: 20mg | Fiber: 7g | Sugars: 12g

4. Quinoa Fruit Bowl

Preparation time: 15 minutes
Servings: 1

Ingredients:

* 1/2 cup cooked quinoa
* 1/2 cup mixed fresh fruits (e.g., berries, diced apple, diced pear)
* 1 tbsp chopped nuts (e.g., almonds, walnuts)
* 1 tbsp unsweetened Greek yogurt
* 1 tsp honey (optional)
* 1/4 tsp ground cinnamon

Instructions:

1. Prepare the quinoa according to the package instructions. Once cooked, let it cool down slightly.
2. In a serving bowl, combine the cooked quinoa, mixed fresh fruits, and chopped nuts.
3. Top the fruit and quinoa mixture with a dollop of unsweetened Greek yogurt.
4. If desired, drizzle honey over the top for added sweetness.
5. Sprinkle ground cinnamon evenly over the bowl.
6. Toss the ingredients gently to mix everything together.
7. Your heart-healthy Quinoa Fruit Bowl is ready to serve!

Nutritional Information (per serving):
Cal: 300 | Carbs: 45g | Pro: 9g | Fat: 10g | Chol: 0mg | Sod: 10mg | Fiber: 7g | Sugars: 15g

5. Almond Banana Smoothie

Preparation time: 5 minutes
Servings: 1

Ingredients:

* 1 ripe banana, peeled and sliced
* 1 cup unsweetened almond milk
* 1 tablespoon almond butter
* 1/2 teaspoon vanilla extract
* 1/4 teaspoon ground cinnamon
* Ice cubes (optional)

Instructions:

1. In a blender, combine the sliced banana, unsweetened almond milk, almond butter, vanilla extract, and ground cinnamon.
2. If you prefer a colder smoothie, you can add a few ice cubes to the blender as well.
3. Blend the ingredients on high speed until the mixture is smooth and creamy.
4. Taste the smoothie and adjust the sweetness or cinnamon to your liking, if necessary.
5. Pour the almond banana smoothie into a glass and serve immediately.

Nutritional Information (per serving):
Cal: 180 | Carbs: 25g | Pro: 5g | Fat: 9g | Chol: 0mg | Sod: 100mg | Fiber: 4g | Sugars: 13g

6. Spinach Omelet Roll

Preparation time: 10 minutes
Servings: 1

Ingredients:

* 2 eggs
* 1 cup fresh spinach leaves, chopped
* 1/4 cup bell peppers, diced
* 1/4 cup onions, diced
* 1/4 cup tomatoes, diced
* 1/4 tsp. pepper
* 1/4 tsp. dried oregano
* Cooking spray

Instructions:

1. In a bowl, whisk the eggs until well beaten.
2. Heat a non-stick skillet over medium heat and coat it with cooking spray.
3. Add the diced bell peppers and onions to the skillet and sauté for 2-3 minutes until they start to soften.
4. Add the chopped spinach leaves and tomatoes to the skillet and sauté for another 2 minutes until the spinach wilts.
5. Pour the beaten eggs into the skillet, spreading them evenly over the vegetables.
6. Sprinkle pepper and dried oregano on top of the omelet.
7. Cook the omelet for 3-4 minutes until the edges are set.
8. Carefully flip the omelet using a spatula and cook for an additional 2-3 minutes until cooked through.
9. Slide the omelet onto a plate, fold it in half, and serve hot.

Nutritional Information (per serving):
Cal: 190 | Carbs: 11g | Pro: 16g | Fat: 10g | Chol: 370mg | Sod: 80mg | Fiber: 3g | Sugars: 5g

7. Greek Yogurt Crunch

Preparation time: 5 minutes
Servings: 1

Ingredients:

* 1/2 cup low-fat Greek yogurt
* 1/4 cup granola (choose low-sugar option)

- 1/4 cup mixed fresh berries (e.g., blueberries, strawberries, raspberries)
- 1 tbsp chopped nuts (e.g., almonds, walnuts)
- 1 tsp honey (optional, for added sweetness)

Instructions:

1. In a serving bowl or glass, start by layering half of the Greek yogurt.
2. Add half of the granola on top of the yogurt.
3. Sprinkle half of the mixed fresh berries over the granola.
4. Add half of the chopped nuts on top of the berries.
5. Repeat the layers with the remaining Greek yogurt, granola, mixed berries, and chopped nuts.
6. Drizzle with honey if desired for added sweetness.
7. Serve immediately and enjoy this heart-healthy Greek Yogurt Crunch!

Nutritional Information (per serving):
Cal: 190 | Carbs: 11g | Pro: 16g | Fat: 10g | Chol: 370mg | Sod: 80mg | Fiber: 3g | Sugars: 5g

8. Apple Cinnamon Pancakes

Preparation time: 10 minutes
Servings: 2

Ingredients:

- 1 cup whole wheat flour
- 2 tsp baking powder
- 1/4 tsp salt
- 1 tsp ground cinnamon
- 1 large egg
- 1 cup low-fat milk
- 1 tbsp honey
- 1 tsp vanilla extract
- 1 apple, peeled and grated
- Cooking spray

Instructions:

1. In a mixing bowl, whisk together the whole wheat flour, baking powder, salt, and ground cinnamon.
2. In a separate bowl, beat the egg and then add the low-fat milk, honey, and vanilla extract. Mix well.
3. Pour the wet ingredients into the dry ingredients and stir until just combined. Avoid overmixing; a few lumps are okay.
4. Gently fold in the grated apple into the pancake batter.
5. Preheat a non-stick skillet over medium heat and lightly coat it with cooking spray.
6. Pour 1/4 cup of pancake batter onto the skillet for each pancake.
7. Cook the pancakes for about 2-3 minutes on each side or until they are golden brown and

cooked through.
8. Repeat the process with the remaining batter.
9. Serve the apple cinnamon pancakes warm with a drizzle of honey or a sprinkle of cinnamon on top.

Nutritional Information (per serving):
Cal: 133 | Carbs: 27g | Pro: 5g | Fat: 1g | Chol: 26mg | Sod: 216mg | Fiber: 3g | Sugars: 8g

9. Oats and Berries Bowl

Preparation time: 5 minutes
Servings: 1

Ingredients:

- 1/2 cup rolled oats
- 1 cup mixed berries (strawberries, blueberries, raspberries)
- 1 tablespoon chopped nuts (almonds, walnuts, or your choice)
- 1 teaspoon honey or maple syrup (optional)
- 1/2 cup low-fat yogurt or plant-based yogurt alternative
- 1/4 teaspoon cinnamon (optional)
- A pinch of salt

Instructions:

1. In a bowl, combine the rolled oats and a pinch of salt. If you prefer your oats softer, you can soak them in water or milk for a few minutes before assembling the bowl.
2. Arrange the mixed berries on top of the oats.
3. Sprinkle the chopped nuts over the berries.
4. If desired, drizzle the honey or maple syrup over the bowl for added sweetness.
5. Spoon the low-fat yogurt or plant-based yogurt on one side of the bowl.
6. If you enjoy the flavor of cinnamon, you can sprinkle a little over the yogurt.
7. Now, your Oats & Berries Bowl is ready to be enjoyed!

Nutritional Information (per serving):
Cal: 300 | Carbs: 45g | Pro: 10g | Fat: 10g | Chol: 0mg | Sod: 150mg | Fiber: 8g | Sugars: 15g

10. Sweet Potato Hash Browns

Preparation time: 15 minutes
Servings: 2

Ingredients:

- 2 medium sweet potatoes, peeled and grated
- 1/4 cup onion, finely chopped
- 1/4 tsp. garlic powder
- 1/4 tsp. paprika

- 1/4 tsp. black pepper
- 1/4 tsp. salt (optional)
- Cooking spray

Instructions:

1. Rinse the grated sweet potatoes under cold water and pat them dry using a clean kitchen towel or paper towels.
2. In a bowl, combine the grated sweet potatoes, chopped onion, garlic powder, paprika, black pepper, and salt (if using). Mix well until the spices are evenly distributed.
3. Heat a non-stick skillet over medium heat and coat it with cooking spray.
4. Divide the sweet potato mixture into two portions. Form each portion into a patty and place it in the skillet.
5. Press down on each patty to flatten it slightly.
6. Cook the hash browns for about 5-6 minutes on each side or until they are golden brown and crispy.
7. Once cooked, transfer the sweet potato hash browns to a plate lined with paper towels to absorb any excess oil.
8. Serve the hash browns hot as a delicious and heart-healthy side dish.

Nutritional Information (per serving):
Cal: 180 | Carbs: 42g | Pro: 2g | Fat: 0g | Chol: 0mg | Sod: 280mg | Fiber: 6g | Sugars: 9g

11. Pesto Egg Wraps

Preparation time: 10 minutes
Servings: 2

Ingredients:

- 4 large eggs
- 2 tablespoons low-fat pesto sauce
- 1 cup baby spinach leaves
- 1/4 cup diced tomatoes
- Cooking spray
- Salt and pepper to taste

Instructions:

1. In a bowl, whisk the eggs until well beaten. Stir in the low-fat pesto sauce until combined.
2. Heat a non-stick skillet over medium heat and coat it with cooking spray.
3. Pour half of the egg mixture into the skillet, spreading it evenly to form a thin layer.
4. Add half of the baby spinach leaves and diced tomatoes onto one half of the egg layer.
5. Season with a pinch of salt and pepper.
6. Fold the empty half of the egg layer over the filling to form a half-moon shape.
7. Cook for 2-3 minutes until the bottom is set.

8. Carefully flip the egg wrap using a spatula and cook for another 1-2 minutes until fully cooked.
9. Repeat the process with the remaining egg mixture and filling ingredients to make the second wrap.
10. Slice each wrap in half and serve hot.

Nutritional Information (per serving):
Cal: 287 | Carbs: 6g | Pro: 18g | Fat: 21g | Chol: 498mg | Sod: 441mg | Fiber: 2g | Sugars: 3g

12. Blueberry Flaxseed Muffins

Preparation time: 15 minutes
Servings: 12 muffins

Ingredients:

- 1 1/2 cups whole wheat flour
- 1/2 cup ground flaxseed
- 1/2 cup unsweetened applesauce
- 1/3 cup honey or maple syrup
- 1/4 cup low-fat plain yogurt
- 2 large eggs
- 1 tsp baking powder
- 1/2 tsp baking soda
- 1/4 tsp salt
- 1 cup fresh or frozen blueberries

Instructions:

1. Preheat your oven to 350°F (175°C). Line a muffin tin with paper liners or lightly grease with cooking spray.
2. In a large mixing bowl, combine the whole wheat flour, ground flaxseed, baking powder, baking soda, and salt. Mix well.
3. In a separate bowl, whisk together the unsweetened applesauce, honey or maple syrup, low-fat plain yogurt, and eggs until well combined.
4. Pour the wet ingredients into the dry ingredients and stir until just combined. Be careful not to overmix.
5. Gently fold in the blueberries into the muffin batter.
6. Divide the batter evenly among the prepared muffin cups, filling each about two-thirds full.
7. Bake the muffins in the preheated oven for 15-18 minutes or until a toothpick inserted into the center of a muffin comes out clean.
8. Remove the muffins from the oven and allow them to cool in the muffin tin for a few minutes before transferring them to a wire rack to cool completely.

Nutritional Information (per serving):
Cal: 160 | Carbs: 23g | Pro: 4g | Fat: 6g | Chol: 32mg | Sod: 135mg | Fiber: 3g | Sugars: 10g

13. Tofu Scramble Fiesta

Preparation time: 15 minutes
Servings: 2

Ingredients:

- 1 block (14 oz) firm tofu, drained and crumbled
- 1/2 cup bell peppers, diced (assorted colors)
- 1/4 cup red onions, diced
- 1/4 cup tomatoes, diced
- 1/4 cup black beans, cooked and drained
- 1/4 cup corn kernels (fresh or frozen)
- 1/2 tsp ground cumin
- 1/4 tsp turmeric powder
- 1/4 tsp chili powder (adjust to taste)
- Salt and pepper to taste
- Cooking spray

Instructions:

1. In a bowl, crumble the drained tofu using a fork, resembling the texture of scrambled eggs.
2. Heat a non-stick skillet over medium heat and coat it with cooking spray.
3. Add the diced bell peppers and red onions to the skillet. Sauté for 2-3 minutes until they start to soften.
4. Stir in the crumbled tofu, ground cumin, turmeric powder, and chili powder. Mix well to evenly distribute the spices.
5. Add the diced tomatoes, black beans, and corn kernels to the skillet. Continue cooking for another 3-4 minutes until the tofu is heated through and the vegetables are tender.
6. Season the tofu scramble with salt and pepper to taste.
7. Divide the Tofu Scramble Fiesta onto plates and serve hot.

Nutritional Information (per serving):
Cal: 250 | Carbs: 19g | Protein: 18g | Fat: 12g | Chol: 0mg | Sod: 400mg | Fiber: 6g | Sugars: 4g

14. Coconut Chia Pudding

Preparation time: 15 minutes
Servings: 2

Ingredients:

- 1/4 cup chia seeds
- 1 cup unsweetened coconut milk
- 1/2 tsp vanilla extract
- 1 tbsp honey or maple syrup (optional, for sweetness)
- Fresh berries and shredded coconut for topping (optional)

Instructions:

1. In a mixing bowl, combine the chia seeds, unsweetened coconut milk, and vanilla extract.
2. If desired, add honey or maple syrup for sweetness and mix well.
3. Stir the mixture thoroughly to ensure the chia seeds are evenly distributed in the coconut milk.
4. Cover the bowl and refrigerate for at least 2 hours or overnight. This allows the chia seeds to absorb the liquid and form a pudding-like consistency.
5. After the chilling period, give the mixture another good stir to break up any clumps that may have formed.
6. Spoon the coconut chia pudding into serving bowls or glasses.
7. Optionally, top the pudding with fresh berries and shredded coconut for added flavor and texture.
8. Serve chilled and enjoy this heart-healthy, low-fat, and low-sodium coconut chia pudding as a delightful and nutritious dessert or breakfast option.

Nutritional Information (per serving):
Cal: 238 | Carbs: 16g | Protein: 4g | Fat: 19g | Chol: 0mg | Sod: 15mg | Fiber: 9g | Sugars: 5g

15. Raspberry Almond Bites

Preparation time: 15 minutes
Servings: 12 bites

Ingredients:

- 1 cup fresh raspberries
- 1 cup unsalted almonds
- 2 tablespoons honey
- 1 teaspoon vanilla extract
- Pinch of salt

Instructions:

1. In a food processor, combine the fresh raspberries, unsalted almonds, honey, vanilla extract, and a pinch of salt.
2. Pulse the ingredients until well combined and the mixture starts to come together.
3. Line a small baking dish or tray with parchment paper.
4. Using your hands, form the mixture into small bite-sized balls and place them on the prepared baking dish.
5. Place the baking dish in the refrigerator and chill the raspberry almond bites for at least 30 minutes to firm up.
6. Once chilled, transfer the bites to an airtight container for storage.
7. Serve and enjoy these heart-healthy Raspberry Almond Bites as a delicious and nutritious snack!

Nutritional Information (per serving):
Cal: 90 | Carbs: 6g | Protein: 2g | Fat: 6g | Chol: 0mg | Sod: 0mg | Fiber: 2g | Sugars: 4g

16. Mushroom Spinach Frittata

Preparation time: 10 minutes
Servings: 4

Ingredients:

- 6 large eggs
- 1 cup fresh spinach, chopped
- 1 cup mushrooms, sliced
- 1/2 cup onions, diced
- 1/2 cup bell peppers, diced
- 1/4 cup low-fat milk
- 1/4 tsp. black pepper
- 1/4 tsp. dried thyme
- 1/4 tsp. garlic powder
- Cooking spray

Instructions:

1. Preheat the oven to 375°F (190°C).
2. In a large bowl, whisk together the eggs, low-fat milk, black pepper, dried thyme, and garlic powder.
3. Heat a non-stick skillet over medium heat and coat it with cooking spray.
4. Add the diced onions and bell peppers to the skillet and sauté for 2-3 minutes until they start to soften.
5. Add the sliced mushrooms to the skillet and sauté for another 2 minutes until they become tender.
6. Stir in the chopped spinach and cook for an additional 1-2 minutes until the spinach wilts.
7. Pour the egg mixture over the vegetables in the skillet, making sure it's evenly distributed.
8. Cook the frittata on the stovetop for 3-4 minutes or until the edges start to set.
9. Transfer the skillet to the preheated oven and bake for 10-12 minutes or until the frittata is fully set and slightly golden on top.
10. Remove the frittata from the oven and let it cool for a minute or two.
11. Cut the frittata into wedges and serve warm.

Nutritional Information (per serving):
Cal: 252 | Carbs: 9g | Protein: 18g | Fat: 16g | Chol: 372mg | Sod: 339mg | Fiber: 2g | Sugars: 4g

17. Pear Walnut Oatmeal

Preparation time: 5 minutes
Servings: 1

Ingredients:

- 1/2 cup rolled oats
- 1 cup water (or milk of your choice)
- 1 ripe pear, diced
- 2 tablespoons chopped walnuts
- 1/2 teaspoon ground cinnamon
- 1 teaspoon honey (optional)

Instructions:

1. In a small saucepan, combine the rolled oats and water (or milk) and bring it to a boil over medium heat.
2. Reduce the heat to low and let the oats simmer for about 3-4 minutes, stirring occasionally until the mixture thickens and the oats are cooked to your desired consistency.
3. Stir in the diced pear, chopped walnuts, and ground cinnamon.
4. If desired, drizzle with honey for added sweetness.
5. Remove the saucepan from the heat and let the oatmeal rest for a minute before serving.
6. Pour the pear walnut oatmeal into a bowl and enjoy it while it's warm.

Nutritional Information (per serving):
Cal: 330 | Carbs: 53g | Protein: 8g | Fat: 12g | Chol: 0mg | Sod: 20mg | Fiber: 8g | Sugars: 19g

18. Breakfast Stuffed Peppers

Preparation time: 15 minutes
Servings: 2

Ingredients:

- 6 large eggs
- 2 large bell peppers (any color), halved and seeds removed
- 4 large eggs
- 1 cup baby spinach, chopped
- 1/2 cup diced tomatoes
- 1/4 cup diced onions
- 1/4 cup diced red bell peppers
- 1/4 tsp. black pepper
- 1/4 tsp. dried oregano
- Cooking spray
- Optional: 2 tbsp. shredded low-fat cheese (for topping)

Instructions:

1. Preheat the oven to 375°F (190°C).
2. In a bowl, beat the eggs until well combined.
3. In a separate bowl, mix together the chopped baby spinach, diced tomatoes, diced onions, and diced red bell peppers.
4. Combine the vegetable mixture with the beaten eggs. Season with black pepper and dried oregano, and mix well.

5. Place the pepper halves on a baking dish, cut-side up.
6. Carefully fill each pepper half with the egg and vegetable mixture until they are almost full.
7. If desired, sprinkle a tablespoon of shredded low-fat cheese over each stuffed pepper.
8. Bake in the preheated oven for about 20 minutes or until the eggs are set and the peppers are slightly tender.
9. Once cooked, remove from the oven and let the stuffed peppers cool for a few minutes.
10. Serve the Breakfast Stuffed Peppers warm and enjoy!

Nutritional Information (per serving):
Cal: 180 | Carbs: 14g | Protein: 12g | Fat: 8g | Chol: 372mg | Sod: 262mg | Fiber: 3g | Sugars: 6g

19. Cranberry Orange Scones

Preparation time: 15 minutes
Servings: 8 scones

Ingredients:

- 2 cups all-purpose flour
- 1/4 cup granulated sugar
- 1 tablespoon baking powder
- 1/4 teaspoon salt
- 1/4 cup cold unsalted butter, cubed
- 1/2 cup dried cranberries
- Zest of 1 orange
- 2/3 cup low-fat milk
- 1 large egg, lightly beaten
- 1 teaspoon vanilla extract

Instructions:

1. Preheat your oven to 400°F (200°C). Line a baking sheet with parchment paper or lightly grease it.
2. In a large bowl, whisk together the flour, granulated sugar, baking powder, and salt.
3. Add the cold butter cubes to the flour mixture. Using a pastry cutter or your fingertips, cut the butter into the flour until the mixture resembles coarse crumbs.
4. Stir in the dried cranberries and orange zest.
5. In a separate bowl, mix together the low-fat milk, lightly beaten egg, and vanilla extract.
6. Pour the milk mixture into the dry ingredients and gently mix until the dough comes together. Be careful not to overmix.
7. Transfer the dough onto a floured surface and shape it into a circle about 1 inch (2.5 cm) thick.
8. Cut the dough into 8 equal wedges.
9. Place the scones on the prepared baking sheet and bake for 12-15 minutes or until the edges are lightly golden.
10. Remove the scones from the oven and let them cool slightly on a wire rack.

11. Serve the Cranberry Orange Scones warm or at room temperature.

Nutritional Information (per serving):
Cal: 206 | Carbs: 30g | Protein: 4g | Fat: 8g | Chol: 40mg | Sod: 268mg | Fiber: 1g | Sugars: 9g

20. Tomato Basil Feta Salad

Preparation time: 10 minutes
Servings: 4

Ingredients:

- 4 large tomatoes, diced
- 1 cup fresh basil leaves, torn
- 1/2 cup crumbled feta cheese
- 1 tbsp extra-virgin olive oil
- 1 tbsp balsamic vinegar
- 1/4 tsp black pepper
- Pinch of salt (optional)

Instructions:

1. In a large mixing bowl, combine the diced tomatoes, torn basil leaves, and crumbled feta cheese.
2. Drizzle the extra-virgin olive oil and balsamic vinegar over the salad.
3. Sprinkle black pepper on top.
4. Gently toss all the ingredients together until well combined.
5. If desired, add a pinch of salt to taste, but keep in mind that feta cheese is already salty, so you may not need much, if any.
6. Transfer the Tomato Basil Feta Salad to a serving dish or individual plates.

Nutritional Information (per serving):
Cal: 110 | Carbs: 6g | Protein: 4g | Fat: 7g | Chol: 20mg | Sod: 170mg | Fiber: 2g | Sugars: 4g

Side Dishes and Appetizers

1. Zesty Avocado Salad Cups

Preparation time: 15 minutes
Servings: 2

Ingredients:

- 2 ripe avocados
- 1 cup cherry tomatoes, halved
- 1/4 cup red onion, finely chopped
- 1/4 cup cucumber, diced
- 2 tbsp fresh cilantro, chopped
- 1 tbsp lime juice
- 1/2 tsp ground cumin
- Salt and pepper to taste

Instructions:

1. Cut the avocados in half and remove the pits. Scoop out the flesh, leaving a thin layer of avocado inside the skins to create avocado cups. Dice the scooped avocado flesh and set it aside.
2. In a bowl, combine the diced avocado, cherry tomatoes, red onion, cucumber, and fresh cilantro.
3. In a small separate bowl, whisk together lime juice, ground cumin, salt, and pepper to make the dressing.
4. Pour the dressing over the avocado mixture and gently toss until everything is well coated.
5. Fill each avocado cup with the zesty avocado salad mixture.
6. Serve immediately as a refreshing and heart-healthy salad.

Nutritional Information (per serving):
Cal: 315 | Carbs: 18g | Pro: 4g | Fat: 28g | Chol: 0mg | Sod: 12mg | Fiber: 10g | Sugars: 4g

2. Quinoa Stuffed Peppers

Preparation time: 15 minutes
Servings: 4

Ingredients:

- 1 cup quinoa, rinsed and drained
- 4 large bell peppers (any color), tops cut off and seeds removed
- 1 cup canned black beans, drained and rinsed
- 1 cup diced tomatoes (canned or fresh)
- 1/2 cup corn kernels (canned, frozen, or fresh)
- 1/2 cup diced zucchini
- 1/4 cup diced red onion
- 2 cloves garlic, minced
- 1 tsp olive oil
- 1 tsp ground cumin
- 1/2 tsp chili powder
- 1/4 tsp paprika
- Salt and pepper to taste
- 1/2 cup shredded reduced-fat cheddar cheese (optional)
- Fresh cilantro for garnish (optional)

Instructions:

1. In a medium saucepan, combine the quinoa with 2 cups of water. Bring to a boil, then reduce the heat to low, cover, and let it simmer for 15 minutes or until the quinoa is cooked and the water is absorbed.
2. While the quinoa is cooking, prepare the bell peppers by removing the tops and seeds. Rinse them under cold water and set aside.
3. In a large skillet, heat the olive oil over medium heat. Add the minced garlic and diced red onion. Sauté for 2-3 minutes until the onion becomes translucent.
4. Add the diced zucchini, black beans, diced tomatoes, and corn kernels to the skillet. Season with ground cumin, chili powder, paprika, salt, and pepper. Cook for an additional 5 minutes until the vegetables are tender.
5. Once the quinoa is ready, add it to the skillet with the vegetable mixture. Stir everything together until well combined.
6. Stuff each bell pepper with the quinoa and vegetable mixture, pressing down gently to fill them.
7. Place the stuffed peppers in a baking dish. If desired, sprinkle shredded reduced-fat cheddar cheese on top of each stuffed pepper.
8. Cover the baking dish with aluminum foil and bake in the preheated oven for 25-30 minutes, or until the peppers are tender.
9. Remove the foil and bake for an additional 5 minutes to melt the cheese (if using).
10. Garnish with fresh cilantro, if desired, before serving.

Nutritional Information (per serving):
Cal: 275 | Carbs: 45g | Pro: 12g | Fat: 5g | Chol: 0mg | Sod: 150mg | Fiber: 8g | Sugars: 6g

3. Lemon Herb Baked Cauliflower

Preparation time: 10 minutes
Servings: 4

Ingredients:

- 1 large head of cauliflower, cut into florets
- 2 tablespoons olive oil
- 2 tablespoons fresh lemon juice
- 1 teaspoon dried oregano
- 1/2 teaspoon dried thyme
- 1/2 teaspoon garlic powder
- 1/4 teaspoon salt
- 1/4 teaspoon black pepper
- Lemon zest from one lemon

Instructions:

1. Preheat your oven to 425°F (220°C) and line a baking sheet with parchment paper.
2. In a large bowl, combine the olive oil, fresh lemon juice, dried oregano, dried thyme, garlic powder, salt, and black pepper. Whisk the ingredients together until well combined.
3. Add the cauliflower florets to the bowl with the lemon-herb mixture. Toss the cauliflower to coat evenly with the marinade.
4. Spread the coated cauliflower evenly on the prepared baking sheet.
5. Bake the cauliflower in the preheated oven for 20-25 minutes or until the cauliflower is tender and slightly browned, stirring once halfway through to ensure even baking.
6. Once the cauliflower is done baking, remove it from the oven and sprinkle lemon zest over the top for an extra burst of flavor.
7. Serve the Lemon-Herb Baked Cauliflower hot as a delightful and heart-healthy side dish.

Nutritional Information (per serving):
Cal: 80 | Carbs: 7g | Protein: 2g | Fat: 6g | Chol: 0mg | Sod: 150mg | Fiber: 3g | Sugars: 3g

4. Cucumber Tomato Bites

Preparation time: 10 minutes
Servings: 4

Ingredients:

- 1 large cucumber
- 1 cup cherry tomatoes
- 2 tbsp low-fat feta cheese, crumbled
- 2 tbsp fresh basil leaves, chopped
- 1 tbsp balsamic vinegar
- 1 tbsp extra-virgin olive oil
- Salt and pepper to taste

Instructions:

1. Wash the cucumber and cherry tomatoes under running water. Pat them dry with a paper towel.
2. Slice the cucumber into thick rounds and arrange them on a serving platter.
3. Cut the cherry tomatoes in half and place them on top of each cucumber slice.
4. Sprinkle the crumbled feta cheese and chopped basil over the cucumber and tomato bites.
5. In a small bowl, whisk together the balsamic vinegar and extra-virgin olive oil to make a simple dressing.
6. Drizzle the dressing over the cucumber tomato bites.
7. Season with a pinch of salt and pepper to taste.
8. Serve immediately as a refreshing and heart-healthy appetizer or snack.

Nutritional Information (per serving):
Cal: 65 | Carbs: 5g | Protein: 2g | Fat: 4g | Chol: 2mg | Sod: 75mg | Fiber: 1g | Sugars: 2g

5. Roasted Garlic Hummus Dip

Preparation time: 10 minutes
Servings: 6

Ingredients:

- 1 can (15 oz) chickpeas (garbanzo beans), drained and rinsed
- 1 whole head of garlic
- 2 tablespoons lemon juice
- 2 tablespoons tahini (sesame paste)
- 2 tablespoons water
- 1/2 teaspoon ground cumin
- 1/4 teaspoon salt
- 1 tablespoon olive oil
- Paprika (for garnish)

Instructions:

1. Preheat the oven to 400°F (200°C).
2. Cut off the top of the whole head of garlic to expose the cloves. Wrap the garlic in aluminum foil and roast it in the preheated oven for about 30 minutes, or until the cloves are soft and golden. Allow it to cool.
3. In a food processor, combine the drained and rinsed chickpeas, roasted garlic cloves (squeeze them out of their skins), lemon juice, tahini, water, ground cumin, and salt.
4. Blend the mixture until smooth and creamy, scraping down the sides of the food processor as needed.
5. If the hummus is too thick, add more water, one tablespoon at a time, until you reach the desired consistency.
6. Transfer the hummus to a serving dish and drizzle olive oil over the top.
7. Sprinkle with a pinch of paprika for garnish.
8. Serve the roasted garlic hummus with sliced veggies, whole grain pita bread, or your favorite heart-healthy dippers.

Nutritional Information (per serving):
Cal: 105 | Carbs: 12g | Protein: 4g | Fat: 5g | Chol: 0mg | Sod: 85mg | Fiber: 3g | Sugars: 0.5g

6. Spinach Mushroom Saute'

Preparation time: 10 minutes
Servings: 2

Ingredients:

- 2 cups fresh spinach leaves

- 1 cup mushrooms, sliced
- 1/4 cup onions, diced
- 1 clove garlic, minced
- 1/4 tsp. black pepper
- 1/4 tsp. dried thyme
- 1/4 tsp. paprika
- Cooking spray

Instructions:

1. Heat a non-stick skillet over medium heat and coat it with cooking spray.
2. Add the diced onions and minced garlic to the skillet and sauté for 1-2 minutes until the onions become translucent.
3. Add the sliced mushrooms to the skillet and sauté for 3-4 minutes until they release their moisture and start to brown.
4. Stir in the fresh spinach leaves and cook for an additional 2-3 minutes until the spinach wilts.
5. Sprinkle black pepper, dried thyme, and paprika over the sautéed vegetables, and toss to combine.
6. Remove the skillet from heat and transfer the Spinach Mushroom Sauté to a serving dish.
7. Serve hot as a delicious and heart-healthy side dish or enjoy it as a light and flavorful main course.

Nutritional Information (per serving):
Cal: 85 | Carbs: 7g | Protein: 5g | Fat: 2g | Chol: 0mg | Sod: 30mg | Fiber: 2g | Sugars: 2g

7. Greek Yogurt Veggie Dip

Preparation time: 10 minutes
Servings: 4

Ingredients:

- 1 cup plain Greek yogurt (low-fat)
- 1/4 cup cucumber, finely grated
- 1/4 cup carrots, grated
- 1/4 cup red bell pepper, finely diced
- 1 clove garlic, minced
- 1/2 tsp. dried dill
- 1/2 tsp. dried parsley
- 1/4 tsp. onion powder
- 1/4 tsp. black pepper
- 1/4 tsp. salt (optional, omit for lower sodium)
- Fresh vegetables (such as sliced cucumbers, carrots, and bell peppers), for serving

Instructions:

1. In a medium bowl, combine the Greek yogurt, grated cucumber, grated carrots, diced red bell pepper, minced garlic, dried dill, dried parsley, onion powder, black pepper, and salt (if using).
2. Mix all the ingredients until well combined.
3. Cover the bowl with plastic wrap and refrigerate

the dip for at least 30 minutes to allow the flavors to meld.
4. Before serving, give the dip a quick stir.
5. Serve the Greek Yogurt Veggie Dip with a platter of fresh vegetables for dipping.

Nutritional Information (per serving):
Cal: 45 | Carbs: 6g | Protein: 5g | Fat: 0g | Chol: 2mg | Sod: 95mg | Fiber: 1g | Sugars: 4g

8. Balsamic Bruschetta Toast

Preparation time: 15 minutes
Servings: 4

Ingredients:

- 4 slices whole-grain baguette or whole wheat bread
- 2 cups fresh tomatoes, diced
- 1/4 cup fresh basil leaves, chopped
- 1 clove garlic, minced
- 1 tbsp balsamic vinegar
- 1 tbsp extra-virgin olive oil
- 1/4 tsp black pepper
- 1/4 tsp salt (optional, or to taste)

Instructions:

1. In a medium bowl, combine the diced tomatoes, chopped basil, minced garlic, balsamic vinegar, extra-virgin olive oil, black pepper, and salt (if using). Mix well to ensure the flavors are well combined. Let the mixture sit for a few minutes to allow the flavors to meld.
2. Preheat your oven's broiler.
3. Place the slices of bread on a baking sheet and lightly toast them under the broiler for about 1-2 minutes on each side or until they turn golden brown. Keep an eye on them to avoid burning.
4. Remove the toasted bread from the oven and set aside.
5. Evenly spoon the balsamic bruschetta mixture onto the toasted bread slices.
6. Serve the Balsamic Bruschetta Toast as a delightful and heart-healthy appetizer or snack.

Nutritional Information (per serving):
Cal: 110 | Carbs: 16g | Protein: 3g | Fat: 4g | Chol: 0mg | Sod: 160mg | Fiber: 2g | Sugars: 2g

9. Steamed Asparagus Spears

Preparation time: 5 minutes
Servings: 4

Ingredients:

- 1 bunch of fresh asparagus spears

- Cooking spray
- 1/4 tsp. garlic powder (optional)
- 1/4 tsp. lemon zest (optional)
- Pinch of salt and pepper

Instructions:

1. Wash the asparagus spears under cold water and trim off the tough ends.
2. Place a steamer basket in a pot and add enough water to reach just below the bottom of the basket. Bring the water to a boil.
3. Add the asparagus spears to the steamer basket, making sure they are evenly spread out.
4. Cover the pot with a lid and steam the asparagus for about 4-5 minutes or until they become tender-crisp. Avoid overcooking to retain their vibrant green color and nutrients.
5. Once done, remove the steamer basket from the pot.
6. If desired, lightly coat the steamed asparagus with cooking spray to add a touch of moisture.
7. Season the asparagus with garlic powder, lemon zest (if using), a pinch of salt, and pepper for added flavor.
8. Serve the steamed asparagus spears as a heart-healthy side dish or as a refreshing addition to salads.

Nutritional Information (per serving):
Cal: 25 | Carbs: 5g | Pro: 2g | Fat: 0g | Chol: 0mg | Sod: 0mg | Fiber: 2g | Sugars: 2g

10. Herbed Chickpea Salad

Preparation time: 15 minutes
Servings: 4

Ingredients:

- 2 cans (15 ounces each) chickpeas (garbanzo beans), drained and rinsed
- 1 cup cucumber, diced
- 1 cup cherry tomatoes, halved
- 1/4 cup red onion, finely chopped
- 1/4 cup fresh parsley, chopped
- 2 tablespoons fresh mint, chopped
- 2 tablespoons fresh lemon juice
- 1 tablespoon extra-virgin olive oil
- 1/4 teaspoon black pepper
- 1/4 teaspoon salt (optional)

Instructions:

1. In a large mixing bowl, combine the chickpeas, cucumber, cherry tomatoes, red onion, parsley, and mint.
2. In a small bowl, whisk together the fresh lemon juice, extra-virgin olive oil, black pepper, and salt (if using).

3. Pour the dressing over the chickpea mixture and gently toss to combine, ensuring all the ingredients are well coated.
4. Refrigerate the salad for at least 30 minutes before serving to allow the flavors to meld.
5. Serve the Herbed Chickpea Salad chilled and enjoy!

Nutritional Information (per serving):
Cal: 190 | Carbs: 25g | Pro: 9g | Fat: 6g | Chol: 0mg | Sod: 20mg | Fiber: 7g | Sugars: 4g

11. Stuffed Portobello Mushrooms

Preparation time: 15 minutes
Servings: 2

Ingredients:

- 2 large Portobello mushrooms
- 1/2 cup cooked quinoa
- 1/4 cup diced bell peppers
- 1/4 cup diced zucchini
- 2 cloves garlic, minced
- 1/4 cup chopped fresh parsley
- 1/4 tsp. dried oregano
- 1/4 tsp. dried basil
- 1/4 tsp. black pepper
- 1/4 cup grated low-fat mozzarella cheese (optional)
- Cooking spray

Instructions:

1. Preheat the oven to 375°F (190°C).
2. Remove the stems from the Portobello mushrooms and gently scrape out the gills to create a hollow space. Chop the mushroom stems finely.
3. In a bowl, combine the chopped mushroom stems, cooked quinoa, diced bell peppers, diced zucchini, minced garlic, chopped parsley, dried oregano, dried basil, and black pepper. Mix well to incorporate all the ingredients.
4. Coat a baking dish with cooking spray and place the Portobello mushroom caps in the dish with the hollow side facing up.
5. Spoon the quinoa and vegetable mixture into each mushroom cap, pressing it down gently to fill the space.
6. If desired, sprinkle grated low-fat mozzarella cheese on top of each stuffed mushroom.
7. Cover the baking dish with aluminum foil and bake in the preheated oven for 15 minutes.
8. Remove the foil and continue baking for an additional 5 minutes or until the mushrooms are tender and the cheese (if added) is melted and slightly golden.
9. Remove from the oven and let the stuffed mushrooms cool for a few minutes before serving.

Nutritional Information (per serving):
Cal: 210 | Carbs: 28g | Protein: 9g | Fat: 7g | Chol: 0mg | Sod: 230mg | Fiber: 4g | Sugars: 4g

12. Beet and Goat Cheese Stack

Preparation time: 15 minutes
Servings: 2

Ingredients:

- 2 medium beets, cooked, peeled, and sliced
- 2 oz goat cheese, crumbled
- 1 cup arugula or mixed greens
- 1 tbsp balsamic vinegar
- 1 tbsp extra-virgin olive oil
- 1/4 tsp black pepper
- 1/4 tsp dried thyme
- Pinch of salt (optional)

Instructions:

1. In a small bowl, whisk together balsamic vinegar, extra-virgin olive oil, black pepper, dried thyme, and a pinch of salt (if desired) to make the dressing.
2. Place a slice of beet on a serving plate or a flat surface.
3. Top the beet slice with a small handful of arugula or mixed greens.
4. Add some crumbled goat cheese on top of the greens.
5. Drizzle a small amount of the dressing over the goat cheese.
6. Repeat the layers with another beet slice, greens, goat cheese, and dressing to create a stack.
7. Finish the stack with a final drizzle of dressing on top.
8. Repeat the process to make a second stack.
9. Serve immediately and enjoy your heart-healthy Beet and Goat Cheese Stack!

Nutritional Information (per serving):
Cal: 160 | Carbs: 10g | Pro: 6g | Fat: 10g | Chol: 20mg | Sod: 180mg | Fiber: 3g | Sugars: 7g

13. Cilantro Lime Quinoa

Preparation time: 15 minutes
Servings: 4

Ingredients:

- 1 cup quinoa
- 2 cups water
- 1/4 cup fresh cilantro, chopped
- 1 lime, juiced
- 1/4 tsp. salt
- 1/4 tsp. black pepper

Instructions:

1. Rinse the quinoa under cold water in a fine-mesh strainer.
2. In a medium saucepan, combine the rinsed quinoa and 2 cups of water.
3. Bring the quinoa to a boil over medium heat. Reduce the heat to low, cover the saucepan with a lid, and let it simmer for 12-15 minutes or until the quinoa is cooked and the water is absorbed.
4. Once the quinoa is cooked, fluff it with a fork.
5. In a separate bowl, combine the fresh cilantro, lime juice, salt, and black pepper.
6. Pour the cilantro lime mixture over the cooked quinoa and toss until well combined.
7. Serve the Cilantro Lime Quinoa warm as a delicious and heart-healthy side dish or as a base for your favorite protein and vegetables.

Nutritional Information (per serving):
Cal: 207 | Carbs: 39g | Protein: 6g | Fat: 2g | Chol: 0mg | Sod: 149mg | Fiber: 4g | Sugars: 1g

14. Heart Healthy Sweet Potato Wedges

Preparation time: 10 minutes
Servings: 4

Ingredients:

- 2 medium sweet potatoes
- 1 tbsp olive oil
- 1/2 tsp paprika
- 1/2 tsp garlic powder
- 1/4 tsp salt (optional)
- Freshly ground black pepper, to taste

Instructions:

1. Preheat your oven to 425°F (220°C) and line a baking sheet with parchment paper.
2. Wash the sweet potatoes thoroughly and cut them into wedges. Try to make them evenly sized for even cooking.
3. In a large bowl, toss the sweet potato wedges with olive oil, paprika, garlic powder, salt (if using), and black pepper. Make sure the wedges are well coated with the seasoning.
4. Spread the seasoned sweet potato wedges in a single layer on the prepared baking sheet.
5. Bake in the preheated oven for about 20-25 minutes or until the sweet potato wedges are tender and lightly browned, flipping them halfway through to ensure even cooking.
6. Once cooked, remove the sweet potato wedges from the oven and let them cool slightly before serving.

Nutritional Information (per serving):
Cal: 172 | Carbs: 32g | Pro: 2g | Fat: 4g | Chol: 0mg | Sod: 137mg | Fiber: 5g | Sugars: 6g

15. Edamame and Tomato Salad

Preparation time: 10 minutes
Servings: 4

Ingredients:

- 2 cups shelled edamame, cooked and cooled
- 1 cup cherry tomatoes, halved
- 1/4 cup red onion, finely chopped
- 2 tbsp fresh parsley, chopped
- 1 tbsp extra-virgin olive oil
- 1 tbsp lemon juice
- 1/2 tsp garlic powder
- Salt and pepper to taste

Instructions:

1. In a large mixing bowl, combine the cooked and cooled edamame, cherry tomatoes, red onion, and fresh parsley.
2. In a small bowl, whisk together the extra-virgin olive oil, lemon juice, garlic powder, salt, and pepper.
3. Pour the dressing over the edamame and tomato mixture, tossing gently to coat all the ingredients.
4. Adjust seasoning if needed, adding more salt and pepper according to your taste preference.
5. Refrigerate the salad for at least 30 minutes to allow the flavors to meld together.
6. Serve the Edamame and Tomato Salad chilled as a refreshing and heart-healthy side dish or light lunch.

Nutritional Information (per serving):
Cal: 150 | Carbs: 11g | Protein: 9g | Fat: 8g | Chol: 0mg | Sod: 75mg | Fiber: 5g | Sugars: 2g

16. Grilled Eggplant Slices

Preparation time: 10 minutes
Servings: 4

Ingredients:

- 2 medium-sized eggplants
- 2 tablespoons olive oil
- 2 cloves garlic, minced
- 1/2 teaspoon dried oregano
- 1/4 teaspoon salt (optional)
- 1/4 teaspoon black pepper
- Fresh lemon wedges, for serving

Instructions:

1. Preheat the grill to medium heat.
2. Wash the eggplants and cut them into 1/2-inch thick slices. If desired, you can peel the skin off the eggplant before slicing.
3. In a small bowl, mix together the olive oil, minced garlic, dried oregano, salt (if using), and black pepper.
4. Brush both sides of the eggplant slices with the olive oil mixture.
5. Place the eggplant slices on the preheated grill. Grill each side for about 3-4 minutes or until tender and grill marks appear.
6. Remove the grilled eggplant slices from the grill and transfer them to a serving plate.
7. Squeeze fresh lemon juice over the grilled eggplant slices before serving for added brightness and flavor.

Nutritional Information (per serving):
Cal: 70 | Carbs: 8g | Pro: 1g | Fat: 5g | Chol: 0mg | Sod: 90mg | Fiber: 4g | Sugars: 3g

17. Avocado Cucumber Salsa

Preparation time: 15 minutes
Servings: 4

Ingredients:

- 1 large avocado, diced
- 1 cup cucumber, diced
- 1/4 cup red onion, finely chopped
- 1/4 cup fresh cilantro, chopped
- 1 small jalapeño, seeds removed and finely chopped
- 2 tablespoons lime juice
- 1 tablespoon olive oil
- Salt and pepper to taste

Instructions:

1. In a medium bowl, combine the diced avocado, cucumber, red onion, cilantro, and jalapeño.
2. Drizzle lime juice and olive oil over the ingredients in the bowl.
3. Gently toss the mixture until all the ingredients are well coated.
4. Season the salsa with salt and pepper to taste.
5. Serve immediately or refrigerate for 30 minutes for the flavors to meld.
6. Enjoy the heart-healthy Avocado Cucumber Salsa with whole-grain tortilla chips or as a refreshing topping for grilled chicken or fish.

Nutritional Information (per serving):
Cal: 105 | Carbs: 8g | Protein: 2g | Fat: 8g | Chol: 0mg | Sod: 5mg | Fiber: 4g | Sugars: 1g

18. Roasted Brussels Sprouts

Preparation time: 10 minutes
Servings: 4

Ingredients:

- 1 lb Brussels sprouts, trimmed and halved
- 2 tbsp olive oil
- 1/4 tsp salt
- 1/4 tsp pepper
- 1/4 tsp garlic powder
- Cooking spray

Instructions:

1. Preheat the oven to 425°F (220°C) and line a baking sheet with aluminum foil. Lightly coat the foil with cooking spray.
2. In a large mixing bowl, toss the halved Brussels sprouts with olive oil, salt, pepper, and garlic powder until they are evenly coated.
3. Spread the Brussels sprouts in a single layer on the prepared baking sheet.
4. Roast the Brussels sprouts in the preheated oven for 20-25 minutes or until they are tender and slightly browned, tossing them halfway through the cooking time for even browning.
5. Once roasted, remove the Brussels sprouts from the oven and transfer them to a serving dish.
6. Serve the roasted Brussels sprouts warm as a delightful and heart-healthy side dish.

Nutritional Information (per serving):
Cal: 90 | Carbs: 10g | Pro: 3g | Fat: 5g | Chol: 0mg | Sod: 155mg | Fiber: 4g | Sugars: 2g

19. Minty Watermelon Cubes

Preparation time: 10 minutes
Servings: 4

Ingredients:

- 4 cups watermelon, diced into cubes
- 2 tbsp fresh mint leaves, finely chopped
- 1 tsp lime juice
- 1/4 tsp black salt (optional)

Instructions:

1. In a large bowl, add the diced watermelon cubes.
2. Sprinkle the chopped mint leaves over the watermelon.
3. Drizzle the lime juice on top and toss gently to combine.
4. If desired, sprinkle a pinch of black salt for added flavor (optional).
5. Refrigerate for at least 10 minutes before serving to let the flavors meld.
6. Serve the refreshing minty watermelon cubes chilled.

Nutritional Information (per serving):
Cal: 46 | Carbs: 11g | Protein: 1g | Fat: 0g | Chol: 0mg | Sod: 53mg | Fiber: 1g | Sugars: 8g

20. Green Pea and Mint Spread

Preparation time: 10 minutes
Servings: 4

Ingredients:

- 1 cup frozen green peas, thawed
- 1/4 cup fresh mint leaves
- 1/4 cup plain Greek yogurt (low-fat)
- 1 tbsp lemon juice
- 1 clove garlic, minced
- 1/4 tsp salt (optional, for heart-healthy diets, consider omitting or reducing)
- 1/4 tsp black pepper
- 1/4 tsp crushed red pepper flakes (optional, adjust to taste)

Instructions:

1. In a food processor or blender, combine the thawed green peas, fresh mint leaves, Greek yogurt, lemon juice, minced garlic, salt (if using), black pepper, and crushed red pepper flakes (if using).
2. Blend the mixture until smooth and creamy, scraping down the sides as needed to ensure everything is well incorporated.
3. Taste and adjust seasoning, adding more salt or pepper if desired.
4. Transfer the Green Pea and Mint Spread to a serving bowl.
5. Serve the spread with whole-grain crackers, sliced vegetables (carrots, cucumbers, bell peppers), or use it as a spread on whole-grain bread or wraps.

Nutritional Information (per serving):
Cal: 70 | Carbs: 10g | Protein: 4g | Fat: 1g | Chol: 1mg | Sod: 59mg | Fiber: 3g | Sugars: 3g

Soups

1. Hearty Lentil Vegetable Soup

Preparation time: 15 minutes
Servings: 4

Ingredients:

- 1 cup dried green lentils, rinsed and drained
- 1 onion, chopped
- 2 carrots, diced
- 2 celery stalks, diced
- 2 cloves garlic, minced
- 1 can (14 oz) diced tomatoes, no salt added
- 4 cups low-sodium vegetable broth
- 1 tsp dried thyme
- 1 tsp dried oregano
- 1 bay leaf
- Salt and pepper to taste
- 2 cups fresh spinach leaves

Instructions:

1. In a large pot, sauté the chopped onion, carrots, and celery over medium heat until softened, about 5 minutes.
2. Add the minced garlic and sauté for another minute until fragrant.
3. Add the rinsed lentils, diced tomatoes, vegetable broth, dried thyme, dried oregano, bay leaf, salt, and pepper. Stir well to combine.
4. Bring the soup to a boil, then reduce the heat to low, cover the pot, and simmer for 20-25 minutes or until the lentils are tender.
5. Stir in the fresh spinach leaves and cook for an additional 2 minutes until the spinach wilts.
6. Remove the bay leaf from the soup and adjust seasoning with more salt and pepper if needed.
7. Ladle the hearty lentil vegetable soup into bowls and serve hot.

Nutritional Information (per serving):
Cal: 190 | Carbs: 35g | Protein: 16g | Fat: 2g | Chol: 0mg | Sod: 80mg | Fiber: 12g | Sugars: 7g

2. Creamy Cauliflower Bisque

Preparation time: 10 minutes
Servings: 4

Ingredients:

- 1 medium cauliflower, chopped into florets
- 1 tablespoon olive oil
- 1 small onion, diced
- 2 garlic cloves, minced
- 4 cups low-sodium vegetable broth
- 1 cup unsweetened almond milk (or any non-dairy milk of your choice)
- 1/2 teaspoon dried thyme
- Salt and pepper, to taste
- Fresh parsley, for garnish (optional)

Instructions:

1. In a large pot, heat the olive oil over medium heat. Add the diced onions and minced garlic, and sauté for about 2-3 minutes until the onions become translucent.
2. Add the cauliflower florets to the pot and stir them with the onions and garlic, allowing them to cook for an additional 2 minutes.
3. Pour in the low-sodium vegetable broth and bring the mixture to a boil. Reduce the heat to a simmer and cover the pot. Let it cook for about 15-20 minutes or until the cauliflower becomes tender.
4. Once the cauliflower is cooked, carefully transfer the mixture to a blender. Blend until smooth and creamy. You can also use an immersion blender directly in the pot.
5. Return the blended mixture to the pot (if you used a regular blender), and stir in the unsweetened almond milk. Season with dried thyme, salt, and pepper. Heat the bisque over low heat for a few more minutes until it's warmed through.
6. Serve the creamy cauliflower bisque in bowls. Garnish with fresh parsley if desired.

Nutritional Information (per serving):
Cal: 140 | Carbs: 17g | Pro: 4g | Fat: 7g | Chol: 0mg | Sod: 180mg | Fiber: 5g | Sugars: 6g

3. Spinach Quinoa Minestrone

Preparation time: 15 minutes
Servings: 4

Ingredients:

- 1 cup quinoa, rinsed
- 4 cups low-sodium vegetable broth
- 1 cup canned crushed tomatoes (low sodium)
- 1 cup chopped spinach
- 1/2 cup diced carrots
- 1/2 cup diced zucchini
- 1/2 cup diced onions
- 2 cloves garlic, minced
- 1 tsp. dried basil
- 1 tsp. dried oregano
- 1/2 tsp. black pepper
- 1/4 tsp. red pepper flakes (optional)
- 1 tbsp. olive oil
- Grated Parmesan cheese for garnish (optional)

Instructions:

1. In a large pot, heat the olive oil over medium heat. Add the diced onions and minced garlic, and sauté until the onions are translucent and fragrant.
2. Add the diced carrots and zucchini to the pot,

and cook for a few minutes until they start to soften.
3. Pour in the low-sodium vegetable broth and crushed tomatoes. Stir in the dried basil, dried oregano, black pepper, and red pepper flakes (if using). Bring the mixture to a boil.
4. Once the soup is boiling, reduce the heat to low and add the rinsed quinoa. Cover the pot and let it simmer for about 15 minutes or until the quinoa is cooked and tender.
5. Stir in the chopped spinach and let it wilt in the soup for a minute or two.
6. Taste the soup and adjust the seasoning if needed.
7. Ladle the Spinach Quinoa Minestrone into serving bowls. If desired, garnish with grated Parmesan cheese.

Nutritional Information (per serving):
Cal: 190 | Carbs: 31g | Pro: 8g | Fat: 5g | Chol: 0mg | Sod: 200mg | Fiber: 5g | Sugars: 5g

4. Tuscan Bean Tomato Soup

Preparation time: 15 minutes
Servings: 4

Ingredients:

- 1 tbsp olive oil
- 1 small onion, diced
- 2 cloves garlic, minced
- 1 carrot, diced
- 1 celery stalk, diced
- 1 can (14 oz) diced tomatoes (low sodium)
- 2 cans (15 oz each) cannellini beans, drained and rinsed
- 4 cups low-sodium vegetable broth
- 1 tsp dried thyme
- 1 tsp dried oregano
- Salt and pepper to taste
- Fresh basil leaves for garnish

Instructions:

1. In a large pot, heat the olive oil over medium heat.
2. Add the diced onion and sauté until translucent, about 3-4 minutes.
3. Stir in the minced garlic and cook for an additional 30 seconds until fragrant.
4. Add the diced carrot and celery to the pot, and cook for another 3-4 minutes until they start to soften.
5. Pour in the low-sodium vegetable broth, diced tomatoes, cannellini beans, dried thyme, and dried oregano. Stir to combine.
6. Bring the soup to a boil, then reduce the heat to low and let it simmer for about 10 minutes, allowing the flavors to meld.

7. Season with salt and pepper to taste.
8. Ladle the Tuscan Bean Tomato Soup into bowls, garnish with fresh basil leaves, and serve hot.

Nutritional Information (per serving):
Cal: 190 | Carbs: 31g | Pro: 12g | Fat: 4g | Chol: 0mg | Sod: 240mg | Fiber: 9g | Sugars: 5g

5. Moroccan Chickpea Stew

Preparation time: 10 minutes
Servings: 4

Ingredients:

- 1 tbsp olive oil
- 1 large onion, chopped
- 2 garlic cloves, minced
- 1 tsp ground cumin
- 1/2 tsp ground coriander
- 1/2 tsp ground cinnamon
- 1/4 tsp ground turmeric
- 1/4 tsp ground ginger
- 1/4 tsp cayenne pepper (optional, adjust to taste)
- 2 cups cooked chickpeas (or 1 can, drained and rinsed)
- 1 can (14 oz) diced tomatoes
- 2 cups low-sodium vegetable broth
- 1 cup chopped carrots
- 1 cup chopped bell peppers (any color)
- 1 cup chopped zucchini
- 1/4 cup chopped dried apricots (optional)
- Salt and pepper to taste
- Fresh cilantro or parsley for garnish

Instructions:

1. In a large pot or Dutch oven, heat the olive oil over medium heat.
2. Add the chopped onion and sauté for about 3 minutes until it becomes translucent.
3. Stir in the minced garlic and cook for an additional minute until fragrant.
4. Add the ground cumin, coriander, cinnamon, turmeric, ground ginger, and cayenne pepper (if using) to the pot. Stir well to coat the onions and garlic with the spices. Cook for another minute to enhance the flavors.
5. Add the cooked chickpeas, diced tomatoes (with their juices), and low-sodium vegetable broth to the pot. Stir to combine all the ingredients.
6. Bring the stew to a simmer and let it cook for about 5 minutes.
7. Add the chopped carrots, bell peppers, and zucchini to the pot. Stir everything together and let the stew simmer for an additional 15-20 minutes or until the vegetables are tender.
8. If using chopped dried apricots, add them to the stew and cook for another 5 minutes to allow the flavors to meld.

9. Season the stew with salt and pepper to taste.
10. Serve the Moroccan Chickpea Stew hot, garnished with fresh cilantro or parsley.

Nutritional Information (per serving):
Cal: 190 | Carbs: 30g | Pro: 8g | Fat: 6g | Chol: 0mg | Sod: 150mg | Fiber: 8g | Sugars: 9g

6. Lemon Herb Chicken Broth

Preparation time: 10 minutes
Servings: 4

Ingredients:

- 4 cups low-sodium chicken broth
- 1 lb boneless, skinless chicken breasts
- 1 lemon, juiced and zested
- 2 cloves garlic, minced
- 1 tsp dried thyme
- 1 tsp dried rosemary
- 1 tsp dried parsley
- 1/4 tsp black pepper
- 1 bay leaf
- 1 cup chopped carrots
- 1 cup chopped celery
- 1 cup chopped onion

Instructions:

1. In a large pot, combine the chicken broth, chicken breasts, lemon juice, lemon zest, minced garlic, thyme, rosemary, parsley, black pepper, and bay leaf.
2. Bring the mixture to a boil over medium-high heat.
3. Reduce the heat to low, cover the pot, and let it simmer for 20 minutes or until the chicken is fully cooked and tender.
4. Remove the chicken from the broth and shred it using two forks.
5. Return the shredded chicken to the pot and add the chopped carrots, celery, and onion.
6. Simmer the broth with the vegetables for an additional 10 minutes or until the vegetables are tender.
7. Remove the bay leaf before serving.

Nutritional Information (per serving):
Cal: 180 | Carbs: 10g | Pro: 24g | Fat: 4g | Chol: 66mg | Sod: 460mg | Fiber: 2g | Sugars: 4g

7. Ginger Carrot Turmeric Soup

Preparation time: 10 minutes
Servings: 4

Ingredients:

- 1 tbsp olive oil
- 1 onion, chopped
- 3 cloves garlic, minced
- 1-inch fresh ginger, grated
- 4 large carrots, peeled and chopped
- 1 tsp ground turmeric
- 4 cups low-sodium vegetable broth
- Salt and pepper to taste
- Fresh cilantro, for garnish (optional)

Instructions:

1. In a large pot, heat the olive oil over medium heat.
2. Add the chopped onion and sauté until it becomes translucent, about 3-4 minutes.
3. Stir in the minced garlic and grated ginger, and cook for an additional 1-2 minutes until fragrant.
4. Add the chopped carrots and ground turmeric to the pot. Stir well to coat the carrots with the spices.
5. Pour in the low-sodium vegetable broth, and bring the mixture to a boil.
6. Reduce the heat to low, cover the pot, and simmer for 15-20 minutes until the carrots are tender.
7. Remove the pot from the heat and let the soup cool slightly.
8. Use an immersion blender or a regular blender to puree the soup until smooth and creamy.
9. Season with salt and pepper to taste.
10. Ladle the Ginger Carrot Turmeric Soup into bowls, and garnish with fresh cilantro, if desired.

Nutritional Information (per serving):
Cal: 120 | Carbs: 17g | Protein: 2g | Fat: 5g | Chol: 0mg | Sod: 80mg | Fiber: 4g | Sugars: 8g

8. Zesty Gazpacho Delight

Preparation time: 15 minutes
Servings: 4

Ingredients:

- 4 large ripe tomatoes, diced
- 1 cucumber, peeled and diced
- 1 bell pepper (red, yellow, or green), diced
- 1 small red onion, finely chopped
- 2 cloves garlic, minced
- 2 cups tomato juice (low sodium)
- 2 tbsp red wine vinegar
- 2 tbsp extra-virgin olive oil
- 1/2 tsp cumin
- 1/2 tsp paprika
- 1/4 tsp cayenne pepper (optional, for extra heat)
- Salt and pepper to taste
- Fresh basil or cilantro leaves for garnish

Instructions:

1. In a large mixing bowl, combine the diced tomatoes, cucumber, bell pepper, red onion, and minced garlic.

2. In a blender or food processor, add half of the tomato juice, red wine vinegar, olive oil, cumin, paprika, cayenne pepper (if using), salt, and pepper. Blend until smooth.
3. Pour the blended mixture into the bowl with the diced vegetables. Add the remaining tomato juice and stir everything together.
4. Cover the bowl and refrigerate the gazpacho for at least 2 hours to allow the flavors to meld together.
5. Before serving, taste the gazpacho and adjust seasoning as needed.
6. Ladle the chilled gazpacho into serving bowls and garnish with fresh basil or cilantro leaves.

Nutritional Information (per serving):
Cal: 90 | Carbs: 12g | Pro: 2g | Fat: 4g | Chol: 0mg | Sod: 50mg | Fiber: 2g | Sugars: 6g

9. Thai Coconut Curry Bisque

Preparation time: 15 minutes
Servings: 4

Ingredients:

- 1 tbsp olive oil
- 1 small onion, finely chopped
- 2 cloves garlic, minced
- 1 tbsp Thai red curry paste
- 2 cups low-sodium vegetable broth
- 1 can (14 oz) light coconut milk
- 2 cups chopped mixed vegetables (carrots, bell peppers, zucchini, etc.)
- 1 cup diced tofu (optional)
- 1 tbsp low-sodium soy sauce
- 1 tsp brown sugar
- 1 lime, juiced
- Salt and pepper to taste
- Fresh cilantro for garnish

Instructions:

1. In a large pot, heat olive oil over medium heat. Add the chopped onion and garlic, and sauté until softened and fragrant.
2. Stir in the Thai red curry paste and cook for another minute to release its flavors.
3. Pour in the low-sodium vegetable broth and bring the mixture to a simmer.
4. Add the light coconut milk and mixed vegetables to the pot. If using tofu, add it now as well.
5. Season the bisque with low-sodium soy sauce, brown sugar, lime juice, salt, and pepper. Stir well to combine all the ingredients.
6. Let the bisque simmer for about 10 minutes, or until the vegetables are tender and the flavors have melded together.
7. Taste the bisque and adjust seasoning as needed.
8. Ladle the Thai Coconut Curry Bisque into serving bowls and garnish with fresh cilantro.

Nutritional Information (per serving):
Cal: 190 | Carbs: 15g | Protein: 5g | Fat: 12g | Chol: 0mg | Sod: 260mg | Fiber: 3g | Sugars: 6g

10. Roasted Red Pepper Chowder

Preparation time: 15 minutes
Servings: 4

Ingredients:

- 2 large red bell peppers
- 1 small onion, diced
- 2 cloves garlic, minced
- 1 medium potato, peeled and diced
- 2 cups low-sodium vegetable broth
- 1 cup low-fat milk
- 1/4 tsp. dried thyme
- 1/4 tsp. paprika
- Salt and pepper to taste
- Fresh chives or parsley for garnish (optional)

Instructions:

1. Preheat the oven to 425°F (220°C). Place the whole red bell peppers on a baking sheet lined with parchment paper. Roast them in the oven for about 20 minutes, turning occasionally, until the skin is charred and blistered. Remove from the oven and let them cool slightly.
2. Once the roasted bell peppers are cool enough to handle, remove the charred skin, seeds, and stems. Chop the roasted peppers into small pieces.
3. In a large pot or saucepan, sauté the diced onion and minced garlic over medium heat until the onion becomes translucent and fragrant.
4. Add the diced potato and chopped roasted red peppers to the pot, stirring them together with the onion and garlic.
5. Pour in the low-sodium vegetable broth and bring the mixture to a boil. Reduce the heat, cover the pot, and let it simmer for about 15 minutes or until the potatoes are tender.
6. Using an immersion blender or regular blender, carefully puree the mixture until smooth. If using a regular blender, work in batches and be cautious of the hot liquid.
7. Return the pureed mixture to the pot and stir in the low-fat milk (or plant-based milk), dried thyme, and paprika. Season with salt and pepper to taste.
8. Cook the chowder for an additional 5 minutes, stirring occasionally, until heated through and well combined.
9. Serve the Roasted Red Pepper Chowder hot, garnished with fresh chives or parsley if desired.

Nutritional Information (per serving):
Cal: 190 | Carbs: 33g | Protein: 7g | Fat: 3g | Chol: 2mg | Sod: 320mg | Fiber: 5g | Sugars: 8g

11. Sweet Potato Leek Bisque

Preparation time: 15 minutes
Servings: 4

Ingredients:

- 2 large sweet potatoes, peeled and diced
- 2 leeks, washed and sliced (white and light green parts only)
- 1 tablespoon olive oil
- 3 cups low-sodium vegetable broth
- 1 cup unsweetened almond milk (or any low-fat milk of your choice)
- 1/2 teaspoon ground cumin
- 1/4 teaspoon ground nutmeg
- Salt and pepper to taste
- Fresh chives, chopped (for garnish, optional)

Instructions:

1. In a large pot, heat the olive oil over medium heat. Add the sliced leeks and sauté for 2-3 minutes until they start to soften.
2. Add the diced sweet potatoes to the pot and continue to sauté for another 3-4 minutes.
3. Pour in the low-sodium vegetable broth and bring the mixture to a boil. Reduce the heat to low, cover the pot, and let it simmer for about 10-12 minutes or until the sweet potatoes are tender.
4. Remove the pot from the heat and let the mixture cool slightly.
5. Using an immersion blender or a regular blender (in batches), puree the sweet potato and leek mixture until smooth.
6. Return the pureed mixture to the pot and place it back on the stove over low heat.
7. Stir in the unsweetened almond milk, ground cumin, and ground nutmeg. Season with salt and pepper to taste.
8. Cook the bisque for another 2-3 minutes, stirring occasionally until it's heated through.
9. Ladle the Sweet Potato Leek Bisque into serving bowls. Garnish with chopped fresh chives if desired.

Nutritional Information (per serving):
Cal: 210 | Carbs: 36g | Pro: 4g | Fat: 6g | Chol: 0mg | Sod: 380mg | Fiber: 5g | Sugars: 10g

12. Greek Lemon Chicken Soup

Preparation time: 15 minutes
Servings: 4

Ingredients:

- 4 cups low-sodium chicken broth
- 2 cups cooked and shredded chicken breast
- 1/2 cup orzo pasta
- 3 large eggs
- 1/3 cup fresh lemon juice
- 2 teaspoons lemon zest
- 1/4 cup chopped fresh dill
- Salt and pepper to taste

Instructions:

1. In a large pot, bring the chicken broth to a simmer over medium heat.
2. Add the cooked and shredded chicken to the pot and let it heat through.
3. Stir in the orzo pasta and cook according to the package instructions until al dente.
4. In a medium bowl, whisk together the eggs, lemon juice, and lemon zest.
5. Slowly ladle about 1 cup of the hot broth from the pot into the egg mixture, whisking constantly to temper the eggs and prevent curdling.
6. Gradually pour the egg mixture back into the pot while stirring continuously.
7. Cook the soup over low heat for another 2-3 minutes, stirring gently, until it thickens slightly.
8. Stir in the chopped dill, and season with salt and pepper to taste.
9. Remove the pot from the heat.
10. Serve the Greek Lemon Chicken Soup hot, garnished with a sprig of dill if desired.

Nutritional Information (per serving):
Cal: 280 | Carbs: 20g | Pro: 24g | Fat: 10g | Chol: 280mg | Sod: 660mg | Fiber: 1g | Sugars: 2g

13. Asparagus Almond Cream Soup

Preparation time: 15 minutes
Servings: 4

Ingredients:

- 1 lb fresh asparagus, trimmed and chopped
- 1 small onion, diced
- 2 garlic cloves, minced
- 2 cups low-sodium vegetable broth
- 1/2 cup unsalted almond butter
- 1 cup unsweetened almond milk
- 1 tbsp olive oil
- Salt and pepper to taste
- Sliced almonds, for garnish
- Fresh parsley, chopped, for garnish

Instructions:

1. In a large pot, heat the olive oil over medium heat. Add the diced onion and minced garlic, and sauté for about 3 minutes until softened.
2. Add the chopped asparagus to the pot and sauté for an additional 2 minutes.
3. Pour in the low-sodium vegetable broth and bring the mixture to a boil. Reduce the heat to low, cover the pot, and let it simmer for 8-10 minutes until

the asparagus is tender.

4. In a small bowl, whisk together the almond butter and unsweetened almond milk until smooth.
5. Carefully transfer the asparagus mixture to a blender or use an immersion blender directly in the pot to puree the soup until smooth.
6. Return the pureed soup to the pot (if using a blender), and stir in the almond butter mixture. Cook over low heat for another 2-3 minutes to combine the flavors.
7. Season the soup with salt and pepper to taste.
8. Ladle the Asparagus Almond Cream Soup into bowls and garnish with sliced almonds and chopped fresh parsley.

Nutritional Information (per serving):
Cal: 319 | Carbs: 18g | Pro: 11g | Fat: 25g | Chol: 0mg | Sod: 336mg | Fiber: 6g | Sugars: 6g

14. Rustic Mushroom Barley Broth

Preparation time: 15 minutes
Servings: 4

Ingredients:

* 1 cup pearl barley
* 6 cups low-sodium vegetable broth
* 1 tbsp olive oil
* 1 onion, finely chopped
* 3 garlic cloves, minced
* 8 oz mushrooms (such as cremini or button), sliced
* 2 carrots, diced
* 2 celery stalks, diced
* 1 tsp dried thyme
* 1 bay leaf
* Salt and pepper to taste
* Fresh parsley, chopped (for garnish)

Instructions:

1. In a large pot, heat the olive oil over medium heat. Add the chopped onions and garlic, and sauté until they become translucent and fragrant.
2. Add the sliced mushrooms to the pot and cook until they release their moisture and start to brown slightly.
3. Stir in the diced carrots and celery, and cook for a few more minutes until they begin to soften.
4. Add the pearl barley to the pot, along with the dried thyme and bay leaf. Stir everything together to combine.
5. Pour in the low-sodium vegetable broth and bring the mixture to a boil. Once boiling, reduce the heat to low, cover the pot, and let it simmer for about 30-35 minutes, or until the barley is tender.
6. Season the broth with salt and pepper to taste.
7. Remove the bay leaf from the pot before serving.
8. Ladle the Rustic Mushroom Barley Broth into bowls and garnish with freshly chopped parsley.

Nutritional Information (per serving):
Cal: 190 | Carbs: 38g | Pro: 6g | Fat: 3g | Chol: 0mg | Sod: 200mg | Fiber: 8g | Sugars: 6g

15. Spicy Black Bean Chili

Preparation time: 15 minutes
Servings: 4

Ingredients:

* 1 can (15 oz) black beans, drained and rinsed
* 1 can (15 oz) diced tomatoes, undrained
* 1 cup low-sodium vegetable broth
* 1 cup bell peppers, diced (assorted colors)
* 1 cup onions, diced
* 2 cloves garlic, minced
* 1 jalapeno pepper, finely chopped (seeds removed for milder heat)
* 1 tbsp olive oil
* 1 tbsp chili powder
* 1 tsp cumin
* 1/2 tsp paprika
* Salt and pepper to taste
* Fresh cilantro, chopped (for garnish, optional)
* Lime wedges (for serving, optional)

Instructions:

1. In a large pot or Dutch oven, heat the olive oil over medium heat.
2. Add the diced onions, bell peppers, minced garlic, and chopped jalapeno to the pot. Sauté for about 3-4 minutes until the vegetables start to soften.
3. Stir in the chili powder, cumin, paprika, salt, and pepper. Cook for another minute until the spices become fragrant.
4. Add the black beans, diced tomatoes, and low-sodium vegetable broth to the pot. Stir well to combine all the ingredients.
5. Bring the mixture to a boil, then reduce the heat to low, cover the pot, and let the chili simmer for about 10 minutes, allowing the flavors to meld together.
6. Taste the chili and adjust the seasonings if needed.
7. Serve the Spicy Black Bean Chili hot, garnished with chopped cilantro and accompanied by lime wedges for squeezing over the chili, if desired.

Nutritional Information (per serving):
Cal: 190 | Carbs: 31g | Pro: 8g | Fat: 5g | Chol: 0mg | Sod: 180mg | Fiber: 10g | Sugars: 6g

16. Cabbage Tomato Detox Soup

Preparation time: 15 minutes
Servings: 4

Ingredients:

- 1 small head of cabbage, chopped
- 2 cups diced tomatoes (canned or fresh)
- 1 onion, diced
- 2 carrots, sliced
- 2 celery stalks, sliced
- 4 cups low-sodium vegetable broth
- 4 cloves garlic, minced
- 1 tsp olive oil
- 1/2 tsp dried thyme
- 1/2 tsp dried oregano
- 1/4 tsp red pepper flakes (optional)
- Salt and pepper to taste
- Fresh parsley for garnish

Instructions:

1. In a large pot, heat the olive oil over medium heat. Add the diced onion and sauté until translucent.
2. Add the minced garlic, dried thyme, dried oregano, and red pepper flakes (if using) to the pot. Stir and cook for another minute.
3. Add the chopped cabbage, carrots, and celery to the pot. Season with salt and pepper to taste. Cook for about 5 minutes, stirring occasionally, until the vegetables start to soften.
4. Pour in the low-sodium vegetable broth and diced tomatoes (with their juice) into the pot. Bring the soup to a boil.
5. Reduce the heat to low, cover the pot, and let the soup simmer for about 10 minutes or until all the vegetables are tender.
6. Taste the soup and adjust the seasoning if needed.
7. Ladle the Cabbage Tomato Detox Soup into bowls, garnish with fresh parsley, and serve hot.

Nutritional Information (per serving):
Cal: 110 | Carbs: 21g | Protein: 5g | Fat: 2g | Chol: 0mg | Sod: 200mg | Fiber: 7g | Sugars: 10g

17. Creamy Avocado Lime Gazpacho

Preparation time: 15 minutes
Servings: 4

Ingredients:

- 2 ripe avocados, peeled and pitted
- 1 cucumber, peeled and chopped
- 1 green bell pepper, chopped
- 1/2 small red onion, chopped
- 2 cloves garlic, minced
- 2 cups low-sodium vegetable broth
- 1/4 cup fresh cilantro leaves
- 1/4 cup fresh lime juice
- 1/4 cup plain Greek yogurt (low-fat)
- 1 tbsp olive oil
- Salt and pepper to taste

Instructions:

1. In a blender or food processor, combine the avocados, cucumber, green bell pepper, red onion, and minced garlic.
2. Add the low-sodium vegetable broth, fresh cilantro leaves, lime juice, and plain Greek yogurt to the blender.
3. Blend all the ingredients until smooth and creamy.
4. If the gazpacho is too thick, you can add a little more vegetable broth to reach your desired consistency.
5. Season the gazpacho with salt and pepper to taste.
6. Transfer the gazpacho to a bowl and cover it. Refrigerate for at least 1 hour to chill and allow the flavors to meld.
7. Before serving, drizzle each bowl with a little olive oil and garnish with additional cilantro leaves if desired.

Nutritional Information (per serving):
Cal: 260 | Carbs: 22g | Protein: 6g | Fat: 19g | Chol: 0mg | Sod: 220mg | Fiber: 9g | Sugars: 6g

18. Red Lentil Butternut Squash Soup

Preparation time: 15 minutes
Servings: 4

Ingredients:

- 1 cup red lentils, rinsed and drained
- 3 cups butternut squash, peeled and diced
- 1 onion, finely chopped
- 2 cloves garlic, minced
- 1 tsp. ground cumin
- 1/2 tsp. ground coriander
- 4 cups low-sodium vegetable broth
- 1 cup water
- Salt and pepper to taste
- 1 tbsp. olive oil
- Fresh cilantro, for garnish (optional)

Instructions:

1. In a large pot, heat the olive oil over medium heat.
2. Add the chopped onion and minced garlic to the pot. Sauté for 2-3 minutes until the onion becomes translucent.
3. Stir in the ground cumin and coriander, and cook for an additional minute until fragrant.

4. Add the diced butternut squash and red lentils to the pot. Stir everything together to coat the vegetables and lentils with the spices.
5. Pour in the low-sodium vegetable broth and water. Bring the mixture to a boil.
6. Reduce the heat to low, cover the pot, and let the soup simmer for about 15 minutes or until the butternut squash and lentils are tender.
7. Once the squash and lentils are cooked, use an immersion blender to puree the soup until smooth. If you don't have an immersion blender, carefully transfer the soup in batches to a regular blender and blend until smooth. Be cautious as the soup will be hot.
8. Season the soup with salt and pepper to taste.
9. Serve the Red Lentil Butternut Squash Soup hot, garnished with fresh cilantro if desired.

Nutritional Information (per serving):
Cal: 289 | Carbs: 47g | Protein: 14g | Fat: 5g | Chol: 0mg | Sod: 251mg | Fiber: 16g | Sugars: 7g

19. Quinoa Kale Harvest Soup

Preparation time: 15 minutes
Servings: 4

Ingredients:

- 1 cup quinoa, rinsed
- 1 tablespoon olive oil
- 1 cup onion, diced
- 2 cloves garlic, minced
- 2 carrots, diced
- 2 celery stalks, diced
- 4 cups low-sodium vegetable broth
- 2 cups water
- 2 cups kale, chopped
- 1 teaspoon dried thyme
- 1/2 teaspoon ground turmeric
- 1/4 teaspoon ground black pepper
- Salt to taste

Instructions:

1. In a large pot, heat the olive oil over medium heat.
2. Add the diced onion and sauté for 2-3 minutes until it becomes translucent.
3. Stir in the minced garlic and sauté for another 30 seconds until fragrant.
4. Add the diced carrots and celery to the pot and cook for 3-4 minutes until they start to soften.
5. Pour in the vegetable broth and water, and bring the mixture to a boil.
6. Add the rinsed quinoa, dried thyme, ground turmeric, and ground black pepper. Stir well.
7. Reduce the heat to low, cover the pot, and let the soup simmer for 10 minutes.
8. Stir in the chopped kale and continue to simmer for an additional 5 minutes until the quinoa is fully

cooked and the kale wilts.
9. Season the soup with salt to taste.
10. Serve the Quinoa Kale Harvest Soup hot, and enjoy!

Nutritional Information (per serving):
Cal: 230 | Carbs: 34g | Pro: 8g | Fat: 8g | Chol: 0mg | Sod: 80mg | Fiber: 6g | Sugars: 5g

20. Artichoke Tomato Basil Bisque

Preparation time: 15 minutes
Servings: 4

Ingredients:

- 1 can (14 oz) artichoke hearts, drained and chopped
- 1 can (14 oz) diced tomatoes, with juice
- 1 onion, finely chopped
- 2 cloves garlic, minced
- 2 cups low-sodium vegetable broth
- 1 cup low-fat milk
- 1/4 cup fresh basil leaves, chopped
- 1/4 tsp dried thyme
- 1/4 tsp dried oregano
- Salt and pepper to taste
- Cooking spray

Instructions:

1. Heat a large pot or saucepan over medium heat. Coat the bottom with cooking spray.
2. Add the chopped onion and minced garlic to the pot. Sauté for 2-3 minutes until the onion becomes translucent.
3. Add the chopped artichoke hearts and diced tomatoes (with their juice) to the pot. Stir and let it cook for another 2 minutes.
4. Pour in the low-sodium vegetable broth and bring the mixture to a simmer. Allow it to cook for about 5 minutes.
5. Reduce the heat to low and add the low-fat milk, dried thyme, dried oregano, salt, and pepper. Stir well and let it simmer for an additional 2 minutes.
6. Remove the pot from the heat and let the soup cool slightly.
7. Using an immersion blender or a regular blender, carefully blend the soup until it reaches a smooth and creamy consistency.
8. Return the bisque to the pot and place it back on low heat.
9. Add the chopped fresh basil to the soup and stir to incorporate.
10. Cook the bisque for another 2-3 minutes until heated through. Serve the Artichoke Tomato Basil Bisque hot in individual bowls.

Nutritional Information (per serving):
Cal: 160 | Carbs: 27g | Pro: 6g | Fat: 2g | Chol: 2mg | Sod: 695mg | Fiber: 8g | Sugars: 12g

Poultry

1. Herb Roasted Chicken Delight

Preparation time: 15 minutes
Servings: 4

Ingredients:

- 4 bone-in, skin-on chicken thighs
- 1 tbsp olive oil
- 1 tsp dried thyme
- 1 tsp dried rosemary
- 1 tsp dried sage
- 1/2 tsp garlic powder
- 1/2 tsp onion powder
- 1/4 tsp black pepper
- 1/4 tsp salt (optional)
- Fresh herbs (such as parsley or basil) for garnish (optional)

Instructions:

1. Preheat your oven to 425°F (220°C).
2. In a small bowl, mix together the dried thyme, rosemary, sage, garlic powder, onion powder, black pepper, and salt (if using).
3. Pat the chicken thighs dry with paper towels.
4. Rub the chicken thighs with olive oil, ensuring they are coated evenly.
5. Sprinkle the herb mixture over the chicken thighs, rubbing it into the skin.
6. Place the seasoned chicken thighs on a baking sheet lined with parchment paper or a lightly greased baking dish.
7. Roast the chicken in the preheated oven for about 25-30 minutes or until the internal temperature reaches 165°F (74°C) and the skin is golden and crispy.
8. Once cooked, remove the chicken from the oven and let it rest for a few minutes.
9. Garnish with fresh herbs, if desired, and serve hot.

Nutritional Information (per serving):
Cal: 340 | Carbs: 1g | Pro: 23g | Fat: 27g | Chol: 140mg | Sod: 360mg | Fiber: 0g | Sugars: 0g

2. Lemon Garlic Grilled Turkey Breast

Preparation time: 10 minutes
Servings: 4

Ingredients:

- 1 lb (450g) turkey breast, boneless and skinless
- 2 tablespoons lemon juice
- 2 cloves garlic, minced
- 1 tablespoon olive oil
- 1 teaspoon dried oregano
- 1/2 teaspoon black pepper
- 1/4 teaspoon salt (optional, reduce or omit for a lower sodium option)

Instructions:

1. In a small bowl, whisk together the lemon juice, minced garlic, olive oil, dried oregano, black pepper, and optional salt.
2. Place the turkey breast in a shallow dish or a resealable plastic bag. Pour the lemon-garlic marinade over the turkey, making sure it is evenly coated. Seal the bag (if using) or cover the dish with plastic wrap, and refrigerate for at least 1 hour, or ideally, overnight to marinate.
3. Preheat the grill to medium-high heat.
4. Remove the turkey breast from the marinade, allowing any excess marinade to drip off.
5. Grill the turkey breast for about 6-8 minutes per side, or until the internal temperature reaches 165°F (74°C) and the turkey is cooked through. The cooking time may vary depending on the thickness of the turkey breast.
6. Once cooked, remove the turkey from the grill and let it rest for a few minutes before slicing.
7. Serve the lemon-garlic grilled turkey breast with your favorite heart-healthy side dishes and enjoy!

Nutritional Information (per serving):
Cal: 170 | Carbs: 2g | Protein: 36g | Fat: 3.5g | Chol: 85mg | Sod: 280mg | Fiber: 0g | Sugars: 0.5g

3. Ginger Lime Glazed Chicken Skewers

Preparation time: 15 minutes
Servings: 4

Ingredients:

- 1 lb boneless, skinless chicken breasts, cut into cubes
- 1/4 cup low-sodium soy sauce
- 2 tablespoons fresh lime juice
- 2 tablespoons honey
- 1 tablespoon grated fresh ginger
- 2 cloves garlic, minced
- 1/4 teaspoon black pepper
- Cooking spray
- 4 wooden or metal skewers

Instructions:

1. In a bowl, combine the low-sodium soy sauce, fresh lime juice, honey, grated ginger, minced garlic, and black pepper. Mix well to create the marinade.
2. Add the cubed chicken to the marinade, making sure all pieces are well coated. Cover the bowl and let it marinate in the refrigerator for at least 30 minutes (or up to 4 hours) to allow the flavors to infuse.
3. If using wooden skewers, soak them in water for about 15 minutes to prevent burning during grilling.

4. Preheat your grill or grill pan over medium-high heat. If using a grill pan, lightly coat it with cooking spray.
5. Thread the marinated chicken cubes onto the skewers, dividing them evenly.
6. Place the chicken skewers on the preheated grill or grill pan. Cook for about 4-5 minutes on each side or until the chicken is cooked through and has a slight char on the edges.
7. While grilling, you can brush any remaining marinade over the chicken skewers to enhance the flavor.
8. Once cooked, remove the skewers from the grill and let them rest for a minute before serving.

Nutritional Information (per serving):
Cal: 215 | Carbs: 10g | Pro: 26g | Fat: 7g | Chol: 73mg | Sod: 582mg | Fiber: 0g | Sugars: 9g

4. Balsamic Basil Stuffed Chicken Breasts

Preparation time: 15 minutes
Servings: 4

Ingredients:

- 4 boneless, skinless chicken breasts
- 1/4 cup reduced-sodium chicken broth
- 2 tbsp balsamic vinegar
- 1/4 cup fresh basil leaves, chopped
- 1/4 cup sun-dried tomatoes, chopped
- 1/4 cup reduced-fat feta cheese, crumbled
- 1/4 tsp salt
- 1/4 tsp black pepper
- Cooking spray

Instructions:

1. Preheat the oven to 375°F (190°C).
2. In a bowl, combine the chicken broth and balsamic vinegar.
3. Make a pocket in each chicken breast by carefully cutting a slit horizontally through the thickest part, but not cutting all the way through.
4. In another bowl, mix the chopped basil, sun-dried tomatoes, and feta cheese.
5. Stuff each chicken breast with the basil, sun-dried tomato, and feta mixture.
6. Sprinkle salt and black pepper evenly on both sides of the chicken breasts.
7. Heat a non-stick skillet over medium-high heat and coat it with cooking spray.
8. Sear the stuffed chicken breasts for about 2 minutes on each side until they are lightly browned.
9. Transfer the seared chicken breasts to a baking dish.
10. Pour the chicken broth and balsamic vinegar mixture over the chicken breasts.
11. Bake in the preheated oven for 15-20 minutes or until the chicken is cooked through and no longer pink in the center.
12. Serve the Balsamic-Basil Stuffed Chicken Breasts with your favorite side dishes.

Nutritional Information (per serving):
Cal: 215 | Carbs: 5g | Pro: 28g | Fat: 8g | Chol: 87mg | Sod: 316mg | Fiber: 1g | Sugars: 3g

5. Dijon Mustard Turkey Tenderloins

Preparation time: 10 minutes
Servings: 4

Ingredients:

- 1 lb turkey tenderloins
- 2 tbsp Dijon mustard
- 1 tbsp honey
- 1 tbsp low-sodium soy sauce
- 1 tsp olive oil
- 1/2 tsp garlic powder
- 1/2 tsp dried thyme
- 1/4 tsp black pepper
- Cooking spray

Instructions:

1. In a bowl, whisk together the Dijon mustard, honey, low-sodium soy sauce, olive oil, garlic powder, dried thyme, and black pepper.
2. Place the turkey tenderloins in a shallow dish and pour the Dijon mustard mixture over them. Make sure the tenderloins are evenly coated with the marinade. Cover the dish and let it marinate in the refrigerator for at least 30 minutes.
3. Preheat the oven to 375°F (190°C).
4. Heat a non-stick skillet over medium-high heat and coat it with cooking spray.
5. Remove the turkey tenderloins from the marinade, allowing any excess marinade to drip off. Reserve the marinade for later.
6. Sear the turkey tenderloins in the skillet for about 2 minutes on each side, or until they develop a golden-brown crust.
7. Transfer the seared turkey tenderloins to a baking dish and brush them with the reserved marinade.
8. Bake the turkey tenderloins in the preheated oven for 15-20 minutes or until they reach an internal temperature of 165°F (74°C) and are no longer pink in the center.
9. Once cooked, remove the turkey tenderloins from the oven and let them rest for a few minutes before slicing.
10. Serve the Dijon Mustard Turkey Tenderloins with your favorite heart-healthy side dishes and enjoy!

Nutritional Information (per serving):
Cal: 213 | Carbs: 5g | Protein: 34g | Fat: 5g | Chol: 84mg | Sod: 375mg | Fiber: 0.5g | Sugars: 4g

6. Paprika Rubbed Roast Chicken Thighs

Preparation time: 10 minutes
Servings: 4

Ingredients:

- 8 bone-in, skinless chicken thighs
- 2 teaspoons sweet paprika
- 1 teaspoon garlic powder
- 1/2 teaspoon onion powder
- 1/2 teaspoon dried thyme
- 1/2 teaspoon ground black pepper
- 1/4 teaspoon cayenne pepper (optional for a spicy kick)
- Cooking spray

Instructions:

1. Preheat your oven to 425°F (220°C).
2. In a small bowl, mix together the sweet paprika, garlic powder, onion powder, dried thyme, black pepper, and cayenne pepper (if using).
3. Pat the chicken thighs dry with paper towels to remove excess moisture.
4. Rub the spice mixture evenly over all sides of the chicken thighs.
5. Heat a large oven-safe skillet or roasting pan over medium-high heat. Coat it with cooking spray.
6. Add the seasoned chicken thighs to the skillet or roasting pan and cook for 2-3 minutes on each side until they develop a golden-brown crust.
7. Transfer the skillet or roasting pan with the chicken thighs to the preheated oven.
8. Roast the chicken thighs for 20-25 minutes or until the internal temperature reaches 165°F (74°C) and the chicken is cooked through.
9. Once done, remove the chicken from the oven and let it rest for a few minutes before serving.
10. Serve the Paprika-Rubbed Roast Chicken Thighs with your favorite heart-healthy side dishes and enjoy!

Nutritional Information (per serving):
Cal: 280 | Carbs: 2g | Pro: 32g | Fat: 17g | Chol: 190mg | Sod: 170mg | Fiber: 1g | Sugars: 0g

7. Rosemary Lemon Grilled Chicken

Preparation time: 10 minutes
Servings: 4

Ingredients:

- 8 chicken drumsticks (about 2 lbs)
- 2 tablespoons fresh rosemary, chopped
- Zest of 1 lemon
- 2 tablespoons lemon juice
- 2 tablespoons olive oil
- 1/4 teaspoon black pepper
- 1/4 teaspoon salt (optional, for those not strictly following a low-sodium diet)
- Cooking spray

Instructions:

1. In a large mixing bowl, combine the chopped rosemary, lemon zest, lemon juice, olive oil, black pepper, and salt (if using). Mix well to create the marinade.
2. Add the chicken drumsticks to the marinade and toss them to coat evenly. Cover the bowl and let the chicken marinate in the refrigerator for at least 30 minutes (for better flavor, you can marinate for up to 4 hours).
3. Preheat the grill to medium-high heat.
4. Remove the chicken drumsticks from the marinade and discard any excess marinade.
5. Spray the grill grates with cooking spray to prevent sticking. Place the drumsticks on the grill and cook for about 5-6 minutes per side or until the chicken is cooked through and has reached an internal temperature of 165°F (75°C).
6. Once the chicken is done, remove it from the grill and let it rest for a few minutes before serving.
7. Serve the Rosemary-Lemon Grilled Chicken Drumsticks with your favorite heart-healthy side dishes and enjoy!

Nutritional Information (per serving):
Cal: 245 | Carbs: 1g | Protein: 21g | Fat: 18g | Chol: 100mg | Sod: 83mg | Fiber: 0g | Sugars: 0g

8. Apricot Glazed Baked Turkey Meatballs

Preparation time: 15 minutes
Servings: 4

Ingredients:

- 1 lb (450g) ground turkey (preferably lean)
- 1/4 cup whole wheat breadcrumbs
- 1/4 cup finely chopped onions
- 1/4 cup finely chopped fresh parsley
- 1 large egg
- 2 cloves garlic, minced
- 1/4 tsp. black pepper
- 1/4 tsp. dried thyme
- 1/4 tsp. dried sage
- 1/4 tsp. paprika
- Cooking spray

For the Apricot Glaze:

- 1/4 cup unsweetened apricot preserves
- 1 tbsp reduced-sodium soy sauce
- 1 tbsp rice vinegar
- 1/2 tsp grated fresh ginger
- 1/4 tsp crushed red pepper flakes (optional)

Instructions:

1. Preheat the oven to 375°F (190°C). Line a baking sheet with parchment paper or lightly grease it with cooking spray.
2. In a large bowl, combine ground turkey, whole wheat breadcrumbs, chopped onions, fresh parsley, egg, minced garlic, black pepper, dried thyme, dried sage, and paprika. Mix well until all ingredients are evenly incorporated.
3. Using your hands, shape the turkey mixture into meatballs, about 1 inch in diameter, and place them on the prepared baking sheet.
4. In a separate small bowl, whisk together apricot preserves, reduced-sodium soy sauce, rice vinegar, grated fresh ginger, and crushed red pepper flakes (if using) to make the apricot glaze.
5. Brush the meatballs with a thin layer of the apricot glaze, reserving some glaze for later.
6. Bake the meatballs in the preheated oven for 15-20 minutes or until they are fully cooked and lightly browned.
7. Remove the meatballs from the oven and brush them with the remaining apricot glaze.
8. Serve the Apricot-Glazed Baked Turkey Meatballs as a delicious and heart-healthy main dish or as an appetizer.

Nutritional Information (per serving):
Cal: 190 | Carbs: 13g | Protein: 18g | Fat: 7g | Chol: 85mg | Sod: 270mg | Fiber: 1g | Sugars: 6g

9. Tandoori Chicken Lettuce Wraps

Preparation time: 20 minutes
Servings: 4

Ingredients:

- 1 lb boneless, skinless chicken breasts, cut into thin strips
- 1 cup plain low-fat yogurt
- 2 tablespoons tandoori spice blend
- 1 tablespoon lemon juice
- 1 teaspoon minced garlic
- 1 teaspoon grated ginger
- 1/4 teaspoon ground black pepper
- 1/4 teaspoon salt (optional)
- 8 large lettuce leaves (such as iceberg or butter lettuce)
- 1 cucumber, thinly sliced
- 1/2 red onion, thinly sliced
- Fresh cilantro leaves, for garnish

Instructions:

1. In a large mixing bowl, combine the plain yogurt, tandoori spice blend, lemon juice, minced garlic, grated ginger, black pepper, and salt (if using). Mix well to create the marinade.

2. Add the chicken strips to the marinade and toss until they are evenly coated. Cover the bowl with plastic wrap and refrigerate for at least 15 minutes, allowing the flavors to infuse.
3. While the chicken is marinating, prepare the lettuce leaves by washing and drying them thoroughly. Pat them gently with paper towels to remove excess moisture.
4. Heat a non-stick skillet over medium-high heat. Add the marinated chicken strips to the skillet and cook for about 5-7 minutes or until the chicken is cooked through and slightly charred.
5. To assemble the lettuce wraps, place a spoonful of the cooked tandoori chicken on each lettuce leaf. Top with cucumber slices and red onion. Garnish with fresh cilantro leaves.
6. Fold the lettuce leaves over the filling to create wraps. Serve immediately and enjoy your heart-healthy Tandoori Chicken Lettuce Wraps!

Nutritional Information (per serving):
Cal: 218 | Carbs: 9g | Pro: 34g | Fat: 4g | Chol: 84mg | Sod: 346mg | Fiber: 2g | Sugars: 6g

10. Pesto Marinated Grilled Turkey Cutlets

Preparation time: 10 minutes
Servings: 4

Ingredients:

- 4 turkey cutlets (about 1 pound)
- 1/4 cup low-sodium pesto sauce
- 1 tbsp olive oil
- 1/4 tsp black pepper
- Cooking spray

Instructions:

1. In a shallow dish, combine the pesto sauce, olive oil, and black pepper.
2. Add the turkey cutlets to the dish and coat them evenly with the pesto marinade. Cover the dish and refrigerate for at least 30 minutes to marinate (for best results, marinate for up to 4 hours).
3. Preheat the grill to medium-high heat. Alternatively, you can use a grill pan or stovetop grill.
4. Remove the turkey cutlets from the marinade, allowing any excess to drip off.
5. Lightly coat the grill or grill pan with cooking spray to prevent sticking.
6. Grill the turkey cutlets for about 3-4 minutes per side, or until they reach an internal temperature of 165°F (74°C) and are no longer pink in the center.
7. Once grilled, remove the turkey cutlets from the heat and let them rest for a couple of minutes.
8. Serve the Pesto-Marinated Grilled Turkey Cutlets with your favorite side dishes or over a bed of mixed greens for a heart-healthy and delicious meal.

Nutritional Information (per serving):
Cal: 220 | Carbs: 2g | Pro: 30g | Fat: 10g | Chol: 70mg | Sod: 230mg | Fiber: 0g | Sugars: 0g

11. Cilantro Lime Chicken and Rice

Preparation time: 15 minutes
Servings: 4

Ingredients:

- 1 lb boneless, skinless chicken breasts, cut into bite-sized pieces
- 1 cup long-grain brown rice
- 2 cups low-sodium chicken broth
- 1/4 cup fresh lime juice
- 2 cloves garlic, minced
- 1/4 cup chopped fresh cilantro
- 1/4 tsp. black pepper
- Cooking spray

Instructions:

1. In a large skillet, heat cooking spray over medium-high heat.
2. Add the chicken pieces and cook until browned and cooked through, about 5-6 minutes. Set aside.
3. In a separate saucepan, combine the brown rice, low-sodium chicken broth, lime juice, and minced garlic. Bring to a boil.
4. Reduce the heat to low, cover, and let the rice simmer for 12-15 minutes or until fully cooked and the liquid is absorbed.
5. Once the rice is cooked, fluff it with a fork and add the cooked chicken to the rice.
6. Stir in the chopped cilantro and black pepper, mixing everything well.
7. Serve the Cilantro-Lime Chicken and Rice hot, garnishing with additional cilantro if desired.

Nutritional Information (per serving):
Cal: 350 | Carbs: 32g | Protein: 30g | Fat: 8g | Chol: 75mg | Sod: 100mg | Fiber: 3g | Sugars: 1g

12. Garlic Herb Roasted Turkey Wings

Preparation time: 15 minutes
Servings: 4

Ingredients:

- 4 turkey wings
- 3 cloves garlic, minced
- 1 tsp dried thyme
- 1 tsp dried rosemary
- 1 tsp dried sage
- 1/2 tsp black pepper
- 1/4 tsp salt

- 2 tbsp olive oil
- Cooking spray

Instructions:

1. Preheat your oven to 375°F (190°C).
2. In a small bowl, mix together the minced garlic, dried thyme, dried rosemary, dried sage, black pepper, salt, and olive oil.
3. Place the turkey wings in a large mixing bowl and pour the garlic-herb mixture over them. Toss the wings until they are evenly coated with the seasoning.
4. Line a baking sheet with aluminum foil and lightly coat it with cooking spray to prevent sticking.
5. Arrange the seasoned turkey wings on the baking sheet in a single layer.
6. Roast the turkey wings in the preheated oven for about 50-60 minutes or until they are cooked through and golden brown, flipping them halfway through the cooking time for even browning.
7. Once fully cooked, remove the turkey wings from the oven and let them rest for a few minutes before serving.
8. Serve the Garlic-Herb Roasted Turkey Wings with your favorite heart-healthy side dishes.

Nutritional Information (per serving):
Cal: 452 | Carbs: 1g | Protein: 40g | Fat: 32g | Chol: 147mg | Sod: 337mg | Fiber: 0g | Sugars: 0g

13. Rosemary Baked Chicken Quarters

Preparation time: 10 minutes
Servings: 4

Ingredients:

- 4 chicken leg quarters (about 1.5 kg)
- 1 large orange, juiced and zested
- 2 tablespoons low-sodium soy sauce
- 2 tablespoons olive oil
- 3 cloves garlic, minced
- 1 tablespoon fresh rosemary, chopped
- 1/2 teaspoon black pepper
- 1/4 teaspoon salt (optional)
- Cooking spray

Instructions:

1. In a large bowl, combine the orange juice, orange zest, low-sodium soy sauce, olive oil, minced garlic, chopped rosemary, black pepper, and optional salt. Mix well to create the marinade.
2. Place the chicken leg quarters in the marinade and coat them thoroughly. Cover the bowl with plastic wrap and refrigerate for at least 30 minutes (or up to 4 hours) to allow the flavors to meld.
3. Preheat your oven to 425°F (220°C).
4. Line a baking dish with aluminum foil and lightly coat it with cooking spray.

5. Remove the chicken leg quarters from the marinade and place them on the prepared baking dish, skin side up.
6. Pour any remaining marinade over the chicken pieces.
7. Bake the chicken in the preheated oven for about 35-40 minutes or until the internal temperature reaches 165°F (74°C) and the chicken is cooked through, with crispy skin.
8. Once done, remove the chicken from the oven and let it rest for a few minutes before serving.

Nutritional Information (per serving):

Cal: 470 | Carbs: 10g | Protein: 32g | Fat: 34g | Chol: 160mg | Sod: 580mg | Fiber: 2g | Sugars: 5g

14. Mediterranean Stuffed Zucchini

Preparation time: 15 minutes
Servings: 4

Ingredients:

- 4 medium zucchinis
- 1 lb lean ground turkey
- 1 cup diced tomatoes
- 1/2 cup diced red bell pepper
- 1/2 cup diced red onion
- 1/4 cup chopped Kalamata olives
- 1/4 cup crumbled feta cheese
- 2 cloves garlic, minced
- 1 tsp dried oregano
- 1 tsp dried basil
- 1/4 tsp black pepper
- 1 tbsp olive oil
- Cooking spray
- Fresh parsley, for garnish

Instructions:

1. Preheat the oven to 375°F (190°C).
2. Cut the zucchinis in half lengthwise and scoop out the centers, creating "boats." Reserve the scooped-out zucchini flesh for later use.
3. In a large skillet, heat the olive oil over medium heat. Add the minced garlic and sauté for about 30 seconds until fragrant.
4. Add the ground turkey to the skillet and cook until browned, breaking it apart with a spatula as it cooks.
5. Stir in the diced tomatoes, red bell pepper, red onion, and the reserved zucchini flesh. Cook for another 2-3 minutes until the vegetables are slightly softened.
6. Add the dried oregano, dried basil, and black pepper to the skillet, and mix well to combine.
7. Remove the skillet from the heat and stir in the chopped Kalamata olives and crumbled feta cheese.
8. Line a baking dish with aluminum foil and lightly coat it with cooking spray. Place the zucchini

boats in the baking dish.
9. Stuff each zucchini boat with the turkey and vegetable mixture, pressing down gently to pack the filling.
10. Cover the baking dish with aluminum foil and bake in the preheated oven for 20 minutes. Then, remove the foil and bake for an additional 10 minutes until the zucchinis are tender and slightly browned.
11. Garnish with fresh parsley and serve hot.

Nutritional Information (per serving):

Cal: 220 | Carbs: 10g | Pro: 24g | Fat: 9g | Chol: 65mg | Sod: 220mg | Fiber: 3g | Sugars: 6g

15. Honey Mustard Glazed Chicken Tenders

Preparation time: 10 minutes
Servings: 4

Ingredients:

- 1 lb (450g) chicken tenders, boneless and skinless
- 2 tablespoons honey
- 2 tablespoons Dijon mustard
- 1 tablespoon low-sodium soy sauce
- 1 tablespoon olive oil
- 1 teaspoon minced garlic
- 1/2 teaspoon dried thyme
- 1/2 teaspoon paprika
- Salt and pepper to taste
- Cooking spray

Instructions:

1. In a bowl, mix together the honey, Dijon mustard, low-sodium soy sauce, olive oil, minced garlic, dried thyme, paprika, salt, and pepper to create the glaze.
2. Place the chicken tenders in a resealable plastic bag and pour half of the glaze over the chicken. Seal the bag and massage the glaze into the chicken to ensure it's evenly coated. Marinate in the refrigerator for at least 30 minutes (or up to 2 hours) for the flavors to meld.
3. Preheat the oven to 400°F (200°C). Line a baking sheet with aluminum foil and lightly coat it with cooking spray.
4. Remove the chicken tenders from the marinade and place them on the prepared baking sheet. Discard the marinade used for coating.
5. Bake the chicken tenders in the preheated oven for about 15-20 minutes, or until they are cooked through and reach an internal temperature of 165°F (74°C).
6. While the chicken is baking, prepare the remaining glaze. Place the reserved glaze in a small saucepan and heat over low heat for a few minutes, stirring constantly until it thickens slightly.
7. Once the chicken tenders are cooked, brush them with the heated glaze for a final touch of

flavor.

8. Serve the Honey-Mustard Glazed Chicken Tenders with your favorite heart-healthy side dishes and enjoy!

Nutritional Information (per serving):
Cal: 220 | Carbs: 11g | Pro: 24g | Fat: 8g | Chol: 75mg | Sod: 280mg | Fiber: 0g | Sugars: 10g

16. Teriyaki Pineapple Turkey Skillet

Preparation time: 15 minutes
Servings: 4

Ingredients:

- 1 lb ground turkey
- 1 cup fresh pineapple chunks
- 1/2 cup low-sodium teriyaki sauce
- 1 red bell pepper, sliced
- 1 green bell pepper, sliced
- 1 small onion, thinly sliced
- 2 cloves garlic, minced
- 1 tbsp vegetable oil
- 1/4 tsp black pepper
- 1/4 tsp crushed red pepper flakes (optional)
- 2 green onions, sliced (for garnish)

Instructions:

1. In a large skillet, heat the vegetable oil over medium-high heat.
2. Add the ground turkey to the skillet and cook, breaking it up with a spatula, until it's no longer pink and fully cooked.
3. Add the sliced red bell pepper, green bell pepper, and onion to the skillet. Sauté for 3-4 minutes until the vegetables start to soften.
4. Stir in the minced garlic and cook for another 1-2 minutes until fragrant.
5. Pour the low-sodium teriyaki sauce over the turkey and vegetables. Mix well to combine.
6. Add the pineapple chunks to the skillet and cook for 2-3 minutes until they are heated through.
7. Season the skillet with black pepper and crushed red pepper flakes (if using), adjusting the spice level to your preference.
8. Once everything is heated through and well combined, remove the skillet from the heat.
9. Serve the Teriyaki Pineapple Turkey Skillet over steamed brown rice or quinoa.

Nutritional Information (per serving):
Cal: 295 | Carbs: 21g | Pro: 24g | Fat: 12g | Chol: 76mg | Sod: 468mg | Fiber: 3g | Sugars: 15g

17. Italian Herb Roasted Chicken Legs

Preparation time: 10 minutes
Servings: 4

Ingredients:

- 8 chicken legs (about 2 lbs)
- 2 tablespoons olive oil
- 2 teaspoons dried basil
- 1 teaspoon dried oregano
- 1 teaspoon garlic powder
- 1/2 teaspoon onion powder
- 1/2 teaspoon paprika
- 1/4 teaspoon black pepper
- Cooking spray

Instructions:

1. Preheat your oven to 425°F (220°C). Line a baking sheet with aluminum foil and lightly coat it with cooking spray.
2. In a small bowl, mix together the dried basil, dried oregano, garlic powder, onion powder, paprika, and black pepper.
3. Pat the chicken legs dry with paper towels and place them on the prepared baking sheet.
4. Drizzle the olive oil over the chicken legs, then sprinkle the herb mixture evenly over them. Gently rub the herbs and oil onto the chicken legs to coat them thoroughly.
5. Arrange the chicken legs in a single layer on the baking sheet.
6. Roast the chicken legs in the preheated oven for 35-40 minutes or until the internal temperature reaches 165°F (74°C) and the skin is crispy and golden.
7. Once cooked, remove the chicken legs from the oven and let them rest for a few minutes before serving.

Nutritional Information (per serving):
Cal: 280 | Carbs: 1g | Pro: 28g | Fat: 18g | Chol: 140mg | Sod: 115mg | Fiber: 0g | Sugars: 0g

18. Lemon Pepper Turkey Breast SlicesLegs

Preparation time: 10 minutes
Servings: 4

Ingredients:

- 1 lb turkey breast slices
- 1 lemon, juiced and zested
- 1 tsp black pepper, freshly ground
- 1/2 tsp garlic powder
- 1/4 tsp salt (optional, for low-sodium diet)
- 1 tbsp olive oil

Instructions:

1. In a bowl, combine the lemon juice, lemon zest, black pepper, garlic powder, and salt (if using) to create the marinade.
2. Place the turkey breast slices in the marinade, making sure they are evenly coated. Let them marinate for at least 5 minutes.
3. Heat olive oil in a non-stick skillet over medium heat.
4. Add the marinated turkey slices to the skillet and cook for about 3-4 minutes per side or until they are fully cooked and reach an internal temperature of 165°F (74°C).
5. Once cooked, transfer the turkey slices to a serving plate.
6. Garnish with some extra lemon zest and freshly ground black pepper if desired.
7. Serve the Lemon-Pepper Turkey Breast Slices with your favorite heart-healthy side dishes and enjoy!

Nutritional Information (per serving):

Cal: 180 | Carbs: 2g | Pro: 33g | Fat: 4g | Chol: 75mg | Sod: 180mg | Fiber: 0g | Sugars: 0g

19. Moroccan Spiced Chicken Stir Fry

Preparation time: 15 minutes
Servings: 2

Ingredients:

- 1 boneless, skinless chicken breast, thinly sliced
- 1 tablespoon olive oil
- 1 teaspoon ground cumin
- 1/2 teaspoon ground cinnamon
- 1/4 teaspoon ground ginger
- 1/4 teaspoon ground turmeric
- 1/4 teaspoon paprika
- 1/4 teaspoon black pepper
- 1/4 teaspoon salt (optional or adjust to taste)
- 1 small onion, thinly sliced
- 1 bell pepper (any color), thinly sliced
- 1 cup broccoli florets
- 1 cup cauliflower florets
- 2 cloves garlic, minced
- 1 tablespoon lemon juice
- Fresh cilantro for garnish (optional)
- Cooked brown rice or quinoa (optional, for serving)

Instructions:

1. In a bowl, combine the sliced chicken with olive oil, ground cumin, ground cinnamon, ground ginger, ground turmeric, paprika, black pepper, and salt (if using). Toss until the chicken is evenly coated with the spices.
2. Heat a large skillet or wok over medium-high heat. Add the spiced chicken and sauté for 3-4

minutes until it starts to brown. Remove the chicken from the skillet and set it aside.
3. In the same skillet, add a little more olive oil if needed. Add the sliced onions and bell pepper, and sauté for 2-3 minutes until they begin to soften.
4. Add the broccoli and cauliflower florets to the skillet and continue to cook for an additional 3-4 minutes until the vegetables are tender-crisp.
5. Stir in the minced garlic and cook for another 30 seconds until fragrant.
6. Return the cooked chicken to the skillet and toss everything together to combine. Cook for an additional minute to heat the chicken through.
7. Drizzle the lemon juice over the stir-fry and give it a final toss.
8. Serve the Moroccan Spiced Chicken Stir-Fry on its own or with cooked brown rice or quinoa for a heart-healthy and satisfying meal. Garnish with fresh cilantro, if desired.

Nutritional Information (per serving):

Cal: 320 | Carbs: 21g | Pro: 28g | Fat: 14g | Chol: 65mg | Sod: 180mg | Fiber: 7g | Sugars: 6g

20. Buffalo Chicken Cauliflower Bites

Preparation time: 15 minutes
Servings: 4

Ingredients:

- 1 medium head of cauliflower, cut into bite-sized florets
- 1 cup cooked chicken breast, shredded
- 1/4 cup hot sauce (choose a low-sodium option)
- 2 tbsp unsalted butter, melted
- 1/2 tsp garlic powder
- 1/4 tsp onion powder
- 1/4 tsp paprika
- Cooking spray

Instructions:

1. Preheat your oven to 425°F (220°C) and line a baking sheet with parchment paper. Lightly coat the paper with cooking spray to prevent sticking.
2. In a large bowl, combine the hot sauce, melted butter, garlic powder, onion powder, and paprika. Mix well to create the buffalo sauce.
3. Add the cauliflower florets and shredded chicken to the bowl with the buffalo sauce. Toss until the cauliflower and chicken are evenly coated.
4. Spread the coated cauliflower and chicken in a single layer on the prepared baking sheet.
5. Bake in the preheated oven for 20-25 minutes or until the cauliflower is tender and slightly crispy at the edges.
6. Remove from the oven and let the Buffalo Chicken Cauliflower Bites cool for a few minutes before serving.

Nutritional Information (per serving):
Cal: 130 | Carbs: 7g | Pro: 10g | Fat: 7g | Chol:
40mg | Sod: 250mg | Fiber: 3g | Sugars: 2g

Beef and Pork

1. Lean Beef Stir Fry

Preparation time: 15 minutes
Servings: 4

Ingredients:

- 1 lb lean beef, thinly sliced
- 2 cups broccoli florets
- 1 red bell pepper, sliced
- 1 yellow bell pepper, sliced
- 1 cup snap peas
- 2 cloves garlic, minced
- 1-inch piece ginger, grated
- 2 tbsp low-sodium soy sauce
- 1 tbsp hoisin sauce
- 1 tbsp cornstarch
- 2 tbsp water
- 1 tbsp vegetable oil

Instructions:

1. In a small bowl, mix the low-sodium soy sauce, hoisin sauce, cornstarch, and water to create the stir-fry sauce. Set aside.
2. In a wok or large skillet, heat the vegetable oil over medium-high heat.
3. Add the minced garlic and grated ginger to the hot oil, and stir-fry for about 30 seconds until fragrant.
4. Add the thinly sliced beef to the wok and cook for 2-3 minutes until it browns slightly. Remove the beef from the wok and set it aside.
5. In the same wok, add the broccoli, bell peppers, and snap peas. Stir-fry for 4-5 minutes until the vegetables are crisp-tender.
6. Return the cooked beef to the wok and pour the stir-fry sauce over the beef and vegetables. Toss everything together to coat evenly.
7. Continue cooking for an additional 1-2 minutes until the sauce thickens and coats the beef and vegetables.
8. Serve the lean beef stir-fry hot over brown rice or quinoa.

Nutritional Information (per serving):
Cal: 230 | Carbs: 15g | Pro: 26g | Fat: 8g | Chol: 65mg | Sod: 340mg | Fiber: 4g | Sugars: 5g

2. Herb Marinated Pork Chops

Preparation time: 10 minutes
Servings: 2

Ingredients:

- 2 boneless pork chops (about 4 ounces each)
- 2 cloves garlic, minced
- 1 tablespoon fresh rosemary, chopped
- 1 tablespoon fresh thyme, chopped
- 1 tablespoon fresh parsley, chopped
- 1 tablespoon olive oil
- 1 tablespoon balsamic vinegar
- 1/4 teaspoon black pepper
- Cooking spray

Instructions:

1. In a bowl, combine minced garlic, chopped rosemary, thyme, parsley, olive oil, balsamic vinegar, and black pepper to make the marinade.
2. Place the pork chops in a resealable plastic bag or shallow dish and pour the marinade over them, ensuring they are evenly coated. Seal the bag or cover the dish and refrigerate for at least 30 minutes, or preferably, marinate overnight for better flavor.
3. Preheat the grill or stovetop grill pan over medium-high heat. Lightly coat the surface with cooking spray.
4. Remove the pork chops from the marinade, allowing any excess to drip off. Discard the remaining marinade.
5. Cook the pork chops for about 4-5 minutes on each side or until they reach an internal temperature of 145°F (63°C). Cooking time may vary depending on the thickness of the chops.
6. Once cooked, transfer the pork chops to a serving plate and let them rest for a couple of minutes before serving.

Nutritional Information (per serving):
Cal: 225 | Carbs: 1g | Pro: 26g | Fat: 12g | Chol: 65mg | Sod: 75mg | Fiber: 0g | Sugars: 0g

3. Zesty Beef Lettuce Wraps

Preparation time: 15 minutes
Servings: 4

Ingredients:

- 1 lb lean ground beef
- 1 tablespoon olive oil
- 1 small onion, finely chopped
- 2 cloves garlic, minced
- 1 red bell pepper, diced
- 1 cup grated carrots
- 1/4 cup low-sodium soy sauce
- 2 tablespoons hoisin sauce
- 1 tablespoon rice vinegar
- 1 teaspoon grated fresh ginger
- 1/4 teaspoon red pepper flakes (optional)
- 1 head of lettuce (such as Bibb or butter lettuce)
- 2 green onions, sliced
- Sesame seeds (optional, for garnish)

Instructions:

1. In a large skillet, heat the olive oil over medium heat. Add the chopped onion and garlic, and

saut for 2-3 minutes until they become translucent.

2. Add the lean ground beef to the skillet and cook until it browns and is no longer pink, breaking it apart with a spatula as it cooks.
3. Stir in the diced red bell pepper and grated carrots. Cook for an additional 3-4 minutes until the vegetables are slightly softened.
4. In a small bowl, mix together the low-sodium soy sauce, hoisin sauce, rice vinegar, grated ginger, and red pepper flakes (if using). Pour the sauce over the beef and vegetables in the skillet, stirring to combine. Let it cook for another 2-3 minutes until everything is well coated in the sauce and heated through.
5. Wash and dry the lettuce leaves, then use them as wraps to serve the zesty beef mixture. Spoon the beef filling onto each lettuce leaf, top with sliced green onions and sesame seeds (if desired), and fold the lettuce around the filling like a burrito.
6. Serve the zesty beef lettuce wraps immediately and enjoy!

Nutritional Information (per serving):
Cal: 275 | Carbs: 10g | Pro: 25g | Fat: 15g | Chol: 70mg | Sod: 440mg | Fiber: 3g | Sugars: 5g

4. Grilled Garlic Pork Tenderloin

Preparation time: 10 minutes
Servings: 4

Ingredients:

* 1 lb pork tenderloin
* 4 cloves garlic, minced
* 1 tbsp low-sodium soy sauce
* 1 tbsp honey
* 1 tbsp olive oil
* 1/2 tsp black pepper
* Cooking spray

Instructions:

1. In a small bowl, combine the minced garlic, low-sodium soy sauce, honey, olive oil, and black pepper to make the marinade.
2. Place the pork tenderloin in a resealable plastic bag and pour the marinade over it. Seal the bag and massage the marinade into the pork, ensuring it's evenly coated. Let it marinate in the refrigerator for at least 30 minutes, or preferably overnight for more flavor.
3. Preheat the grill to medium-high heat and lightly coat it with cooking spray to prevent sticking.
4. Remove the pork tenderloin from the marinade and discard the marinade. Place the pork on the grill and cook for about 15-20 minutes, turning occasionally, until the internal temperature reaches 145°F (63°C). Cooking time may vary depending

on the thickness of the tenderloin.
5. Once cooked, transfer the grilled pork tenderloin to a cutting board and let it rest for a few minutes before slicing.
6. Slice the pork tenderloin into thin pieces and serve immediately. You can pair it with a side of steamed vegetables or a fresh green salad for a complete and heart-healthy meal.

Nutritional Information (per serving):
Cal: 180 | Carbs: 6g | Pro: 25g | Fat: 6g | Chol: 75mg | Sod: 170mg | Fiber: 0g | Sugars: 5g

5. Spicy Beef and Vegetable Soup

Preparation time: 15 minutes
Servings: 4

Ingredients:

* 1 lb lean beef, thinly sliced
* 1 tbsp olive oil
* 1 onion, chopped
* 2 garlic cloves, minced
* 1 bell pepper, diced
* 2 carrots, sliced
* 2 celery stalks, sliced
* 4 cups low-sodium beef broth
* 1 can (14 oz) diced tomatoes, undrained
* 1 tsp cumin
* 1/2 tsp chili powder
* 1/4 tsp cayenne pepper (adjust to taste)
* Salt and pepper to taste
* Fresh cilantro, chopped (for garnish)

Instructions:

1. In a large pot, heat olive oil over medium heat. Add the sliced beef and cook until browned. Remove the beef from the pot and set it aside.
2. In the same pot, add chopped onions and minced garlic. Sauté for a few minutes until they become translucent.
3. Add diced bell pepper, sliced carrots, and sliced celery to the pot. Cook for another 5 minutes, stirring occasionally.
4. Pour in the low-sodium beef broth and add the undrained diced tomatoes. Stir in cumin, chili powder, cayenne pepper, salt, and pepper. Bring the soup to a boil.
5. Once the soup is boiling, reduce the heat to low, cover the pot, and let it simmer for about 15 minutes until the vegetables are tender.
6. Return the browned beef to the pot and let it simmer for an additional 5 minutes to allow the flavors to meld together.
7. Taste the soup and adjust seasoning if needed.
8. Ladle the Spicy Beef and Vegetable Soup into serving bowls, garnish with fresh chopped cilantro, and serve hot.

Nutritional Information (per serving):
Cal: 270 | Carbs: 14g | Pro: 24g | Fat: 12g | Chol: 60mg | Sod: 480mg | Fiber: 4g | Sugars: 7g

6. Citrus Glazed Pork Skewers

Preparation time: 15 minutes
Servings: 4

Ingredients:

- 1 lb (450g) lean pork loin, cut into cubes
- 1/4 cup freshly squeezed orange juice
- 2 tablespoons freshly squeezed lime juice
- 1 tablespoon honey
- 1 tablespoon low-sodium soy sauce
- 2 cloves garlic, minced
- 1/2 teaspoon grated fresh ginger
- 1/4 teaspoon black pepper
- Cooking spray
- 4 metal or soaked wooden skewers

Instructions:

1. In a bowl, combine the orange juice, lime juice, honey, low-sodium soy sauce, minced garlic, grated ginger, and black pepper. Mix well to create the citrus glaze.
2. Place the cubed pork in a resealable plastic bag or a shallow dish and pour half of the citrus glaze over it. Seal the bag or cover the dish and marinate the pork in the refrigerator for at least 30 minutes, allowing the flavors to infuse.
3. Preheat the grill or grill pan over medium heat. If using wooden skewers, make sure to soak them in water for at least 30 minutes to prevent them from burning.
4. Thread the marinated pork cubes onto the skewers.
5. Lightly coat the grill or grill pan with cooking spray to prevent sticking. Place the pork skewers on the grill and cook for about 4-5 minutes per side, or until the pork is cooked through and has reached a safe internal temperature of 145°F (63°C).
6. While grilling, brush the remaining citrus glaze over the pork skewers to add extra flavor and caramelization.
7. Once the pork is fully cooked and glazed, remove the skewers from the grill.
8. Serve the Citrus-Glazed Pork Skewers with your favorite heart-healthy side dishes or over a bed of brown rice or quinoa.

Nutritional Information (per serving):
Cal: 200 | Carbs: 8g | Pro: 25g | Fat: 7g | Chol: 65mg | Sod: 140mg | Fiber: 0g | Sugars: 7g

7. Beef and Broccoli Bake

Preparation time: 15 minutes
Servings: 4

Ingredients:

- 1 lb lean beef, thinly sliced
- 4 cups broccoli florets
- 1 onion, thinly sliced
- 2 cloves garlic, minced
- 1 cup low-sodium beef broth
- 2 tbsp low-sodium soy sauce
- 1 tbsp cornstarch
- 1/4 tsp black pepper
- Cooking spray

Instructions:

1. Preheat the oven to 375°F (190°C). Lightly grease a baking dish with cooking spray.
2. In a large non-stick skillet, cook the thinly sliced beef over medium-high heat until browned. Set aside.
3. In the same skillet, add the minced garlic and sliced onions. Sauté for 2-3 minutes until the onions become translucent.
4. Add the broccoli florets to the skillet and continue cooking for an additional 3-4 minutes until they become tender-crisp.
5. In a small bowl, whisk together the low-sodium beef broth, low-sodium soy sauce, cornstarch, and black pepper until well combined.
6. Pour the sauce mixture into the skillet with the vegetables. Stir and cook for another 1-2 minutes until the sauce thickens.
7. Add the cooked beef back to the skillet and toss everything together until the beef and vegetables are evenly coated with the sauce.
8. Transfer the beef and broccoli mixture to the prepared baking dish, spreading it out evenly.
9. Bake in the preheated oven for 15 minutes to allow the flavors to meld and the dish to heat through.
10. Serve the heart-healthy Beef and Broccoli Bake hot with brown rice or whole-grain noodles, if desired.

Nutritional Information (per serving):
Cal: 270 | Carbs: 12g | Pro: 29g | Fat: 10g | Chol: 70mg | Sod: 260mg | Fiber: 3g | Sugars: 4g

8. Apple Cider Pork Medallions

Preparation time: 15 minutes
Servings: 4

Ingredients:

- 1 lb pork tenderloin, cut into medallions

- 1/2 cup apple cider
- 1 tbsp olive oil
- 2 cloves garlic, minced
- 1 tsp dried thyme
- 1/2 tsp ground cinnamon
- Salt and pepper, to taste
- 2 medium apples, thinly sliced
- 1 tbsp fresh parsley, chopped (for garnish, optional)

Instructions:

1. In a bowl, combine the apple cider, olive oil, minced garlic, dried thyme, ground cinnamon, salt, and pepper. Mix well to make the marinade.
2. Place the pork medallions in a resealable plastic bag or shallow dish. Pour the marinade over the pork, making sure all pieces are coated. Seal the bag or cover the dish and refrigerate for at least 30 minutes to marinate.
3. Heat a large non-stick skillet over medium-high heat. Add the marinated pork medallions to the skillet, reserving the marinade.
4. Cook the pork for 3-4 minutes on each side until browned and cooked through. Remove the pork from the skillet and set aside.
5. In the same skillet, add the sliced apples and cook for 2-3 minutes until they soften slightly.
6. Pour the reserved marinade into the skillet with the apples. Bring it to a simmer and let it cook for 2-3 minutes to thicken slightly.
7. Return the cooked pork medallions to the skillet with the apples and sauce. Toss everything together to coat the pork with the apple cider glaze.
8. Serve the Apple Cider Pork Medallions hot, garnished with fresh chopped parsley if desired.

Nutritional Information (per serving):
Cal: 245 | Carbs: 12g | Pro: 24g | Fat: 10g | Chol: 75mg | Sod: 65mg | Fiber: 2g | Sugars: 9g

9. Balsamic Glazed Beef Kabobs

Preparation time: 15 minutes
Servings: 4

Ingredients:

- 1 lb lean beef (sirloin or tenderloin), cut into 1-inch cubes
- 1/4 cup balsamic vinegar
- 2 tablespoons olive oil
- 2 cloves garlic, minced
- 1 tablespoon low-sodium soy sauce
- 1 tablespoon honey
- 1 teaspoon Dijon mustard
- 1/2 teaspoon black pepper
- 1 red bell pepper, cut into chunks
- 1 green bell pepper, cut into chunks

- 1 red onion, cut into chunks
- 8 cherry tomatoes
- 8 wooden or metal skewers

Instructions:

1. In a bowl, whisk together the balsamic vinegar, olive oil, minced garlic, low-sodium soy sauce, honey, Dijon mustard, and black pepper to make the marinade.
2. Place the beef cubes in a resealable plastic bag or a shallow dish. Pour the marinade over the beef, making sure all pieces are coated. Seal the bag or cover the dish and refrigerate for at least 30 minutes, or preferably, marinate overnight for maximum flavor.
3. If you are using wooden skewers, soak them in water for about 30 minutes to prevent them from burning on the grill.
4. Preheat the grill to medium-high heat.
5. Thread the marinated beef, bell peppers, red onion, and cherry tomatoes onto the skewers, alternating the ingredients.
6. Grill the kabobs for about 10-12 minutes, turning occasionally, or until the beef reaches your desired level of doneness and the vegetables are tender-crisp.
7. Remove the kabobs from the grill and let them rest for a few minutes before serving.

Nutritional Information (per serving):
Cal: 280 | Carbs: 13g | Pro: 24g | Fat: 14g | Chol: 70mg | Sod: 190mg | Fiber: 2g | Sugars: 8g

10. Savory Stuffed Pork Loin

Preparation time: 15 minutes
Servings: 4

Ingredients:

- 1 pound boneless pork loin
- 1 cup fresh spinach leaves
- 1/2 cup low-sodium chicken broth
- 1/4 cup chopped sun-dried tomatoes (rehydrated in water)
- 2 cloves garlic, minced
- 1/4 cup low-fat feta cheese, crumbled
- 1/4 teaspoon dried thyme
- 1/4 teaspoon dried rosemary
- 1/4 teaspoon black pepper
- Cooking twine
- Cooking spray

Instructions:

1. Preheat the oven to 375°F (190°C).
2. Butterfly the pork loin by making a horizontal cut through the center, leaving about 1/2 inch uncut on one side. Open the pork loin like a book.

In a skillet over medium heat, sauté the minced garlic until fragrant. Add the fresh spinach leaves and cook until wilted.

3. Add the chopped sun-dried tomatoes, dried thyme, dried rosemary, and black pepper to the skillet. Stir to combine and cook for an additional 1-2 minutes.
4. Lay the cooked spinach and tomato mixture evenly over the opened pork loin.
5. Sprinkle the crumbled feta cheese on top of the spinach and tomato mixture.
6. Carefully roll up the pork loin, starting from one side. Secure the roll with cooking twine, tying it at regular intervals to keep the stuffing in place.
7. Place the stuffed pork loin on a baking sheet coated with cooking spray.
8. Pour the low-sodium chicken broth into the baking sheet around the pork loin.
9. Roast the stuffed pork loin in the preheated oven for about 30-35 minutes or until the internal temperature reaches 145°F (63°C).
10. Once cooked, remove the pork loin from the oven and let it rest for a few minutes before slicing.
11. Slice the stuffed pork loin, and serve it with the pan juices as a flavorful sauce.

Nutritional Information (per serving):
Cal: 225 | Carbs: 4g | Pro: 28g | Fat: 9g | Chol: 80mg | Sod: 190mg | Fiber: 1g | Sugars: 2g

11. Beef and Spinach Casserole

Preparation time: 15 minutes
Servings: 4

Ingredients:

- 1 lb lean ground beef
- 2 cups fresh spinach, chopped
- 1 cup low-sodium beef broth
- 1 cup low-fat milk
- 1/4 cup whole wheat flour
- 1/4 cup grated Parmesan cheese
- 1/4 cup chopped onions
- 2 garlic cloves, minced
- 1/4 tsp black pepper
- 1/4 tsp dried thyme
- 1/4 tsp dried oregano
- Cooking spray

Instructions:

1. Preheat the oven to 375°F (190°C).
2. In a large skillet, cook the lean ground beef over medium-high heat until browned. Drain any excess fat.
3. Add the chopped onions and minced garlic to the skillet with the beef. Cook for an additional 2-3 minutes until the onions are softened.

1. Stir in the chopped spinach and cook for 1-2 minutes until the spinach wilts.
2. Sprinkle the whole wheat flour over the beef and spinach mixture, stirring to coat evenly.
3. Slowly pour in the low-sodium beef broth and low-fat milk while stirring continuously to create a smooth sauce.
4. Add the black pepper, dried thyme, and dried oregano to the skillet. Mix well.
5. Cook the mixture for another 2-3 minutes until the sauce thickens slightly.
6. Transfer the beef and spinach mixture to a lightly greased casserole dish.
7. Sprinkle grated Parmesan cheese over the top of the casserole.
8. Bake in the preheated oven for 15-20 minutes or until the cheese is melted and bubbly.
9. Remove from the oven and let it cool for a few minutes before serving.

Nutritional Information (per serving):
Cal: 280 | Carbs: 9g | Pro: 26g | Fat: 15g | Chol: 70mg | Sod: 350mg | Fiber: 2g | Sugars: 3g

12. BBQ Pulled Pork Sliders

Preparation time: 15 minutes
Servings: 4

Ingredients:

- 1 pound lean pork tenderloin, trimmed of visible fat
- 1 cup low-sodium BBQ sauce
- 1/2 cup low-sodium chicken or vegetable broth
- 1 tablespoon apple cider vinegar
- 1 tablespoon honey
- 1/2 teaspoon garlic powder
- 1/2 teaspoon onion powder
- 1/2 teaspoon paprika
- 1/4 teaspoon black pepper
- 8 whole wheat slider buns
- 1 cup shredded cabbage or coleslaw mix (optional, for topping)

Instructions:

1. Place the pork tenderloin in a slow cooker.
2. In a mixing bowl, combine the BBQ sauce, chicken or vegetable broth, apple cider vinegar, honey, garlic powder, onion powder, paprika, and black pepper. Stir well to make the sauce.
3. Pour the sauce over the pork tenderloin in the slow cooker, ensuring it is fully coated.
4. Cover the slow cooker and cook the pork on low heat for 6-8 hours or on high heat for 3-4 hours until the pork is tender and easily shreds with a fork.
5. Once the pork is cooked, remove it from the slow cooker, and shred it using two forks.
6. Return the shredded pork to the slow cooker, mix

it with the sauce, and let it sit for another 10-15 minutes to absorb the flavors.

7. To serve, place a generous amount of the BBQ pulled pork on each whole wheat slider bun. If desired, top with shredded cabbage or coleslaw for added crunch and freshness.

Nutritional Information (per serving):
Cal: 350 | Carbs: 39g | Pro: 28g | Fat: 9g | Chol: 60mg | Sod: 450mg | Fiber: 4g | Sugars: 13g

13. Greek Style Beef Tacos

Preparation time: 15 minutes
Servings: 4

Ingredients:

- 1 lb lean ground beef
- 1 cup diced tomatoes
- 1/2 cup diced cucumber
- 1/4 cup diced red onion
- 1/4 cup crumbled feta cheese
- 2 tbsp chopped fresh parsley
- 1 tbsp olive oil
- 1 tbsp red wine vinegar
- 1 tsp dried oregano
- 1/2 tsp garlic powder
- 1/4 tsp black pepper
- 8 small whole wheat or corn tortillas

Instructions:

1. In a large skillet, cook the lean ground beef over medium-high heat until fully browned and cooked through. Drain any excess fat and set aside.
2. In a bowl, combine the diced tomatoes, cucumber, red onion, feta cheese, chopped parsley, olive oil, red wine vinegar, dried oregano, garlic powder, and black pepper. Mix well to make the Greek-style salsa.
3. Warm the whole wheat or corn tortillas in a separate dry skillet over medium heat for about 1 minute per side until pliable.
4. To assemble the tacos, spoon the cooked ground beef onto each tortilla. Top with a generous amount of the Greek-style salsa.
5. Serve the Greek-Style Beef Tacos immediately and enjoy!

Nutritional Information (per serving):
Cal: 380 | Carbs: 28g | Pro: 27g | Fat: 16g | Chol: 75mg | Sod: 480mg | Fiber: 5g | Sugars: 4g

14. Gingered Pork Stir Fry

Preparation time: 15 minutes
Servings: 4

Ingredients:

- 1 lb lean pork loin, thinly sliced
- 2 cups broccoli florets
- 1 red bell pepper, sliced
- 1 cup snow peas
- 1 tablespoon fresh ginger, minced
- 3 cloves garlic, minced
- 2 tablespoons low-sodium soy sauce
- 1 tablespoon rice vinegar
- 1 tablespoon honey
- 1 tablespoon cornstarch
- 2 tablespoons water
- 2 tablespoons canola oil
- 2 green onions, sliced (for garnish)
- Sesame seeds (for garnish)
- Cooked brown rice (optional, for serving)

Instructions:

1. In a small bowl, mix the low-sodium soy sauce, rice vinegar, honey, cornstarch, and water to create the sauce. Set it aside.
2. In a large skillet or wok, heat 1 tablespoon of canola oil over medium-high heat.
3. Add the sliced pork to the skillet and stir-fry until it's browned and cooked through. Remove the pork from the skillet and set it aside.
4. In the same skillet, add the remaining 1 tablespoon of canola oil.
5. Add the minced ginger and garlic to the skillet and stir-fry for about 1 minute until fragrant.
6. Add the broccoli, red bell pepper, and snow peas to the skillet. Stir-fry for 3-4 minutes until the vegetables are tender-crisp.
7. Return the cooked pork to the skillet and pour in the sauce. Stir everything together and let it cook for an additional 1-2 minutes until the sauce thickens and coats the ingredients.
8. Remove the skillet from the heat.
9. Serve the Gingered Pork Stir-Fry over cooked brown rice (optional), and garnish with sliced green onions and sesame seeds.

Nutritional Information (per serving):
Cal: 280 | Carbs: 17g | Pro: 25g | Fat: 11g | Chol: 60mg | Sod: 320mg | Fiber: 3g | Sugars: 8g

15. Mediterranean Beef Skewers

Preparation time: 15 minutes
Servings: 4

Ingredients:

- 1 pound lean beef sirloin, cut into 1-inch cubes
- 1 red bell pepper, cut into chunks
- 1 yellow bell pepper, cut into chunks
- 1 red onion, cut into chunks
- 1 zucchini, sliced

- 2 tablespoons olive oil
- 2 tablespoons lemon juice
- 2 cloves garlic, minced
- 1 teaspoon dried oregano
- 1 teaspoon dried thyme
- 1/2 teaspoon ground black pepper
- 4 wooden or metal skewers

Instructions:

1. If using wooden skewers, soak them in water for at least 30 minutes to prevent burning during cooking.
2. In a large bowl, combine the olive oil, lemon juice, minced garlic, dried oregano, dried thyme, and ground black pepper. Mix well to create the marinade.
3. Add the beef cubes to the marinade, making sure they are evenly coated. Cover the bowl and let it marinate in the refrigerator for at least 1 hour (or preferably overnight) to enhance the flavors.
4. Preheat the grill or a grill pan over medium-high heat.
5. Thread the marinated beef cubes, along with the bell peppers, onion, and zucchini, onto the skewers in an alternating pattern.
6. Place the assembled skewers on the preheated grill and cook for about 10-12 minutes, turning occasionally, or until the beef is cooked to your desired doneness and the vegetables are tender-crisp.
7. Once cooked, remove the skewers from the grill and let them rest for a minute.
8. Serve the Mediterranean Beef Skewers with a side of whole-grain couscous or quinoa, and a fresh salad.

Nutritional Information (per serving):
Cal: 280 | Carbs: 10g | Pro: 27g | Fat: 14g | Chol: 70mg | Sod: 60mg | Fiber: 3g | Sugars: 5g

16. Cranberry Glazed Pork Roast

Preparation time: 15 minutes
Servings: 4

Ingredients:

- 1 (2-pound) boneless pork loin roast
- 1 cup fresh or frozen cranberries
- 1/4 cup pure maple syrup
- 1/4 cup reduced-sodium soy sauce
- 2 tablespoons Dijon mustard
- 2 cloves garlic, minced
- 1/2 teaspoon dried thyme
- 1/2 teaspoon black pepper

Instructions:

1. Preheat the oven to 350°F (175°C). Place the pork loin roast in a roasting pan or baking dish.

2. In a blender or food processor, combine the cranberries, maple syrup, soy sauce, Dijon mustard, minced garlic, dried thyme, and black pepper. Blend until smooth.
3. Pour the cranberry glaze over the pork roast, making sure to coat it evenly.
4. Cover the roasting pan with foil and roast in the preheated oven for about 1 hour.
5. After 1 hour, remove the foil and baste the pork with the pan juices. Continue roasting for an additional 20-30 minutes, or until the internal temperature of the pork reaches 145°F (63°C) and the glaze is slightly caramelized.
6. Remove the roast from the oven and let it rest for a few minutes before slicing.
7. Serve the Cranberry-Glazed Pork Roast with the pan juices drizzled on top.

Nutritional Information (per serving):
Cal: 290 | Carbs: 15g | Pro: 30g | Fat: 10g | Chol: 75mg | Sod: 320mg | Fiber: 2g | Sugars: 10g

17. Teriyaki Beef Lettuce Cups

Preparation time: 15 minutes
Servings: 4

Ingredients:

- 1 lb lean beef, thinly sliced
- 1/4 cup low-sodium teriyaki sauce
- 1 tablespoon low-sodium soy sauce
- 2 cloves garlic, minced
- 1 teaspoon grated fresh ginger
- 1 tablespoon honey
- 1 tablespoon rice vinegar
- 1 tablespoon sesame oil
- 1/4 cup water
- 1 tablespoon cornstarch
- 1 head of iceberg lettuce, leaves separated and washed
- 1/4 cup shredded carrots
- 2 green onions, thinly sliced
- 1 tablespoon sesame seeds (optional)
- Cooking spray

Instructions:

1. In a bowl, mix together the teriyaki sauce, low-sodium soy sauce, minced garlic, grated ginger, honey, rice vinegar, sesame oil, and water.
2. In a separate small bowl, dissolve the cornstarch in 2 tablespoons of cold water, and then add it to the teriyaki sauce mixture. Stir well to combine.
3. Heat a non-stick skillet over medium-high heat and lightly coat it with cooking spray.
4. Add the thinly sliced beef to the skillet and cook for 2-3 minutes until browned.
5. Pour the teriyaki sauce mixture over the beef and continue cooking for another 2-3 minutes until the beef is fully cooked and the sauce thickens.

6. Remove the skillet from the heat and let the beef cool slightly.
7. To assemble the lettuce cups, take a lettuce leaf, add a small amount of the teriyaki beef, top with shredded carrots, sliced green onions, and sprinkle with sesame seeds (optional).
8. Repeat with the remaining lettuce leaves and filling.
9. Serve the Teriyaki Beef Lettuce Cups immediately, and enjoy!

Nutritional Information (per serving):
Cal: 245 | Carbs: 10g | Pro: 24g | Fat: 11g | Chol: 58mg | Sod: 372mg | Fiber: 2g | Sugars: 7g

18. Apricot Glazed Pork Tenderloin

Preparation time: 15 minutes
Servings: 4

Ingredients:

- 1 lb (450g) pork tenderloin
- 1/2 cup unsweetened apricot preserves
- 2 tbsp low-sodium soy sauce
- 2 cloves garlic, minced
- 1/2 tsp ground ginger
- 1/4 tsp black pepper
- Cooking spray

Instructions:

1. Preheat the oven to 400°F (200°C).
2. In a small bowl, mix together the apricot preserves, low-sodium soy sauce, minced garlic, ground ginger, and black pepper.
3. Place the pork tenderloin in a shallow dish and pour half of the apricot glaze over the meat, turning to coat it evenly. Reserve the other half of the glaze for basting.
4. Heat a non-stick skillet over medium-high heat and coat it with cooking spray.
5. Sear the pork tenderloin for 2-3 minutes on each side until it gets a golden brown color.
6. Transfer the seared pork tenderloin to a baking dish and brush it with the reserved apricot glaze.
7. Bake the pork tenderloin in the preheated oven for about 15-20 minutes or until it reaches an internal temperature of 145°F (63°C) and is no longer pink in the center.
8. While the pork is baking, you can baste it with the glaze occasionally to add more flavor and moisture.
9. Once cooked, let the pork rest for a few minutes before slicing it into medallions.
10. Serve the Apricot-Glazed Pork Tenderloin with your favorite heart-healthy side dishes and enjoy!

Nutritional Information (per serving):
Cal: 245 | Carbs: 17g | Pro: 23g | Fat: 8g | Chol: 75mg | Sod: 220mg | Fiber: 0g | Sugars: 14g

19. Beef and Sweet Potato Hash

Preparation time: 15 minutes
Servings: 4

Ingredients:

- 1 lb lean ground beef
- 2 medium sweet potatoes, peeled and diced
- 1/2 cup onion, diced
- 1 red bell pepper, diced
- 1 clove garlic, minced
- 1/2 tsp paprika
- 1/2 tsp dried thyme
- 1/4 tsp salt
- 1/4 tsp black pepper
- Cooking spray

Instructions:

1. In a large non-stick skillet, cook the lean ground beef over medium heat until browned and cooked through. Drain any excess fat and set aside.
2. In the same skillet, add a light coating of cooking spray and sauté the diced sweet potatoes, onions, and red bell pepper until they begin to soften, about 5-7 minutes.
3. Add the minced garlic, paprika, dried thyme, salt, and black pepper to the skillet. Stir well to combine the spices with the vegetables.
4. Return the cooked ground beef to the skillet and mix it with the vegetables. Cook for an additional 3-4 minutes to allow the flavors to meld.
5. Once the sweet potatoes are tender and the ingredients are well combined, remove the skillet from the heat.
6. Serve the Beef and Sweet Potato Hash warm and enjoy a heart-healthy, flavorful meal!

Nutritional Information (per serving):
Cal: 300 | Carbs: 23g | Pro: 23g | Fat: 11g | Chol: 70mg | Sod: 260mg | Fiber: 4g | Sugars: 7g

20. Pineapple Pork Stir Fry

Preparation time: 15 minutes
Servings: 4

Ingredients:

- 1 lb (450g) lean pork, thinly sliced
- 2 cups pineapple chunks (fresh or canned in juice), drained
- 1 red bell pepper, sliced
- 1 green bell pepper, sliced
- 1 small onion, thinly sliced
- 2 garlic cloves, minced
- 1/4 cup low-sodium soy sauce
- 2 tbsp rice vinegar
- 1 tbsp honey

- 1 tsp grated fresh ginger
- 1/4 tsp red pepper flakes (optional)
- 2 tbsp vegetable oil
- 2 cups cooked brown rice, for serving
- Fresh cilantro, for garnish (optional)
- Sesame seeds, for garnish (optional)

Instructions:

1. In a small bowl, mix together the low-sodium soy sauce, rice vinegar, honey, grated ginger, and red pepper flakes (if using). Set the sauce aside.
2. Heat 1 tablespoon of vegetable oil in a large skillet or wok over medium-high heat.
3. Add the sliced pork to the skillet and stir-fry for 4-5 minutes until it's browned and cooked through. Remove the pork from the skillet and set it aside.
4. In the same skillet, add another tablespoon of vegetable oil and sauté the minced garlic until fragrant.
5. Add the sliced onions and bell peppers to the skillet. Stir-fry for 2-3 minutes until the vegetables start to soften.
6. Return the cooked pork to the skillet and add the pineapple chunks.
7. Pour the prepared sauce over the pork and vegetables. Stir everything together and cook for an additional 2 minutes until the sauce coats the ingredients.
8. Remove the skillet from heat.
9. Serve the Pineapple Pork Stir-Fry over cooked brown rice.

Nutritional Information (per serving):
Cal: 345 | Carbs: 34g | Pro: 25g | Fat: 11g | Chol: 55mg | Sod: 486mg | Fiber: 3g | Sugars: 18g

Fish and Seafood

1. Zesty Citrus Salmon Bake

Preparation time: 10 minutes
Servings: 4

Ingredients:

- 4 salmon fillets (4-6 ounces each)
- 1 tablespoon olive oil
- 2 tablespoons fresh lemon juice
- 2 tablespoons fresh orange juice
- 1 teaspoon lemon zest
- 1 teaspoon orange zest
- 2 cloves garlic, minced
- 1/2 teaspoon dried oregano
- 1/2 teaspoon dried thyme
- Salt and pepper, to taste
- Lemon slices and fresh herbs for garnish (optional)

Instructions:

1. Preheat your oven to 400°F (200°C). Line a baking dish with parchment paper or lightly grease it with olive oil to prevent sticking.
2. In a small bowl, mix together the olive oil, lemon juice, orange juice, lemon zest, orange zest, minced garlic, dried oregano, dried thyme, salt, and pepper.
3. Place the salmon fillets in the prepared baking dish, skin-side down. Pour the zesty citrus marinade over the salmon, making sure each fillet is well coated. You can also use a brush to evenly spread the marinade.
4. Let the salmon marinate for about 10 minutes at room temperature to allow the flavors to infuse.
5. Bake the salmon in the preheated oven for 12-15 minutes or until the salmon is cooked through and flakes easily with a fork. The exact cooking time will depend on the thickness of your salmon fillets.
6. Once done, remove the salmon from the oven and garnish with lemon slices and fresh herbs, if desired.
7. Serve the Zesty Citrus Salmon Bake hot with your favorite side dishes or a fresh green salad.

Nutritional Information (per serving):
Cal: 280 | Carbs: 2g | Pro: 28g | Fat: 17g | Chol: 75mg | Sod: 80mg | Fiber: 0g | Sugars: 1g

2. Shrimp and Veggie Skewers

Preparation time: 15 minutes
Servings: 4

Ingredients:

- 1 lb (450g) large shrimp, peeled and deveined
- 1 red bell pepper, cut into chunks
- 1 yellow bell pepper, cut into chunks
- 1 zucchini, sliced into rounds
- 1 red onion, cut into chunks
- 2 tbsp olive oil
- 2 cloves garlic, minced
- 1 tsp paprika
- 1/2 tsp black pepper
- 1/4 tsp salt (optional)
- Wooden or metal skewers

Instructions:

1. If using wooden skewers, soak them in water for at least 30 minutes to prevent burning.
2. In a large bowl, combine the shrimp, bell peppers, zucchini, and red onion.
3. In a separate small bowl, mix together olive oil, minced garlic, paprika, black pepper, and salt (if using).
4. Pour the olive oil mixture over the shrimp and veggies. Toss well to coat everything evenly. Let it marinate for about 10 minutes.
5. Preheat the grill or grill pan over medium-high heat.
6. Thread the marinated shrimp and veggies onto the skewers, alternating between shrimp and vegetables.
7. Grill the skewers for about 2-3 minutes per side or until the shrimp turns pink and opaque.
8. Remove the skewers from the grill and serve immediately.

Nutritional Information (per serving):
Cal: 200 | Carbs: 8g | Pro: 22g | Fat: 8g | Chol: 160mg | Sod: 240mg | Fiber: 2g | Sugars: 4g

3. Tilapia with Lemon Herb Sauce

Preparation time: 10 minutes
Servings: 2

Ingredients:

- 2 tilapia fillets (about 4-6 ounces each)
- 1 tablespoon olive oil
- 1 tablespoon lemon juice
- 1 teaspoon fresh thyme leaves (or 1/2 teaspoon dried thyme)
- 1 teaspoon fresh parsley, chopped
- 1/4 teaspoon garlic powder
- 1/4 teaspoon black pepper
- 1/8 teaspoon salt (optional)
- Lemon slices for garnish (optional)

Instructions:

1. Preheat the oven to 375°F (190°C).
2. In a small bowl, mix together the olive oil, lemon juice, thyme, parsley, garlic powder, black pepper, and salt (if using).
3. Place the tilapia fillets on a baking sheet lined with parchment paper or aluminum foil.
4. Brush the lemon herb sauce over the tilapia fillets,

coating them evenly on both sides.
5. Bake the tilapia in the preheated oven for about 12-15 minutes or until the fish is cooked through and flakes easily with a fork.
6. Remove the tilapia from the oven and let it rest for a minute.
7. Serve the tilapia with lemon slices on top for garnish (if desired).

Nutritional Information (per serving):
Cal: 218 | Carbs: 1g | Pro: 27g | Fat: 11g | Chol: 55mg | Sod: 106mg | Fiber: 0g | Sugars: 0g

4. Grilled Garlic Prawns

Preparation time: 15 minutes
Servings: 2

Ingredients:

- 12 large prawns, peeled and deveined
- 2 cloves garlic, minced
- 1 tablespoon olive oil
- 1 tablespoon fresh lemon juice
- 1/4 teaspoon black pepper
- 1/4 teaspoon paprika
- 1/4 teaspoon red pepper flakes (optional)
- Fresh parsley, chopped, for garnish
- Lemon wedges, for serving

Instructions:

1. In a bowl, combine minced garlic, olive oil, lemon juice, black pepper, paprika, and red pepper flakes (if using).
2. Add the prawns to the marinade and toss until they are evenly coated. Let them marinate for at least 10 minutes.
3. Preheat the grill to medium-high heat.
4. Thread the marinated prawns onto skewers for easy grilling.
5. Place the prawn skewers on the preheated grill and cook for about 2-3 minutes per side or until they turn pink and opaque.
6. Once cooked, remove the prawn skewers from the grill and garnish with chopped fresh parsley.
7. Serve the Grilled Garlic Prawns with lemon wedges on the side.

Nutritional Information (per serving):
Cal: 146 | Carbs: 1g | Pro: 20g | Fat: 7g | Chol: 190mg | Sod: 235mg | Fiber: 0g | Sugars: 0g

5. Baked Dijon Cod Fillets

Preparation time: 10 minutes
Servings: 2

Ingredients:

- 2 cod fillets (about 4-6 ounces each)
- 2 tbsp Dijon mustard
- 1 tbsp lemon juice
- 1/2 tsp garlic powder
- 1/2 tsp dried thyme
- 1/4 tsp black pepper
- Cooking spray

Instructions:

1. Preheat your oven to 400°F (200°C) and line a baking sheet with parchment paper or lightly coat it with cooking spray.
2. In a small bowl, mix the Dijon mustard, lemon juice, garlic powder, dried thyme, and black pepper together to make the marinade.
3. Place the cod fillets on the prepared baking sheet.
4. Spoon the marinade evenly over the top of each cod fillet, spreading it with the back of the spoon to coat the surface.
5. Let the cod fillets marinate for about 5 minutes to enhance the flavors.
6. Bake the cod fillets in the preheated oven for 12-15 minutes or until the fish is cooked through and flakes easily with a fork.
7. Once done, remove the cod fillets from the oven and let them rest for a minute before serving.
8. Plate the Baked Dijon Cod Fillets and pair them with your favorite heart-healthy side dishes like steamed vegetables or quinoa.

Nutritional Information (per serving):
Cal: 187 | Carbs: 3g | Pro: 33g | Fat: 3g | Chol: 75mg | Sod: 280mg | Fiber: 0g | Sugars: 1g

6. Seared Tuna Steaks with Salsa

Preparation time: 15 minutes
Servings: 2

Ingredients:

- 2 tuna steaks (about 6 ounces each)
- 1 tbsp olive oil
- 1/4 tsp salt
- 1/4 tsp black pepper
- 1 cup diced tomatoes
- 1/4 cup diced red onions
- 1/4 cup diced cucumber
- 1/4 cup chopped fresh cilantro
- 1 jalapeno, seeds removed and minced
- 1 tbsp lime juice
- 1/4 tsp cumin

Instructions:

1. In a bowl, combine the diced tomatoes, red onions, cucumber, cilantro, jalapeno, lime juice, and cumin to make the salsa. Mix well and set

aside.

2. Pat dry the tuna steaks with paper towels. Season both sides of the tuna steaks with salt and black pepper.
3. In a non-stick skillet, heat the olive oil over medium-high heat.
4. Add the tuna steaks to the skillet and sear for about 2-3 minutes on each side, or until the tuna reaches your desired level of doneness. For a heart-healthy option, aim for medium-rare to medium doneness.
5. Once cooked, remove the tuna steaks from the skillet and let them rest for a minute.
6. Slice the tuna steaks and serve them with the prepared salsa on top.

Nutritional Information (per serving):
Cal: 256 | Carbs: 7g | Pro: 35g | Fat: 10g | Chol: 55mg | Sod: 325mg | Fiber: 2g | Sugars: 4g

7. Poached Halibut in Broth

Preparation time: 10 minutes
Servings: 2

Ingredients:

- 2 halibut fillets (about 6 ounces each)
- 2 cups low-sodium vegetable broth
- 1 cup water
- 1/2 cup sliced carrots
- 1/2 cup sliced celery
- 1/4 cup chopped onion
- 2 garlic cloves, minced
- 1 bay leaf
- 1/4 tsp. black pepper
- Fresh parsley for garnish (optional)

Instructions:

1. In a medium-sized pot, combine the low-sodium vegetable broth, water, sliced carrots, sliced celery, chopped onion, minced garlic, bay leaf, and black pepper.
2. Bring the broth to a gentle simmer over medium heat.
3. Carefully add the halibut fillets to the simmering broth.
4. Cover the pot and let the halibut poach in the broth for about 8-10 minutes or until the fish is cooked through and flakes easily with a fork.
5. Once the halibut is cooked, carefully remove the fillets from the broth using a slotted spoon and transfer them to serving plates.
6. Discard the bay leaf from the broth.
7. Ladle the poaching broth over the halibut fillets.
8. Garnish with fresh parsley, if desired.
9. Serve the Poached Halibut in Broth with your favorite heart-healthy side dishes like steamed vegetables or quinoa.

Nutritional Information (per serving):
Cal: 185 | Carbs: 7g | Pro: 30g | Fat: 3.5g | Chol: 55mg | Sod: 250mg | Fiber: 2g | Sugars: 3g

8. Lemon Pepper Trout Fillets

Preparation time: 10 minutes
Servings: 2

Ingredients:

- 2 trout fillets (about 4-6 ounces each)
- 1 lemon, thinly sliced
- 1/2 teaspoon lemon zest
- 1 teaspoon freshly ground black pepper
- 1/4 teaspoon salt (optional for a low-sodium version)
- 1 tablespoon olive oil
- Fresh parsley, for garnish (optional)

Instructions:

1. Preheat the oven to 400°F (200°C). Line a baking sheet with parchment paper.
2. Rinse the trout fillets under cold water and pat them dry with paper towels.
3. Place the trout fillets on the prepared baking sheet.
4. Lay lemon slices on top of each fillet, covering the surface.
5. In a small bowl, mix together the lemon zest and freshly ground black pepper.
6. Sprinkle the lemon pepper mixture evenly over the lemon slices on the fillets. Add a pinch of salt if desired, or omit it for a low-sodium version.
7. Drizzle the olive oil over the fillets to keep them moist while baking.
8. Bake the trout fillets in the preheated oven for about 12-15 minutes or until the fish flakes easily with a fork.
9. Once cooked, remove the fillets from the oven and garnish with fresh parsley if desired.
10. Serve the Lemon Pepper Trout Fillets with a side of steamed vegetables or a light salad for a heart-healthy and delicious meal.

Nutritional Information (per serving):
Cal: 220 | Carbs: 1g | Pro: 24g | Fat: 14g | Chol: 80mg | Sod: 100mg | Fiber: 0g | Sugars: 0g

9. Coconut Curry Shrimp Stir Fry

Preparation time: 15 minutes
Servings: 2

Ingredients:

- 8 oz (225g) shrimp, peeled and deveined
- 1 cup broccoli florets

- 1/2 red bell pepper, thinly sliced
- 1/2 yellow bell pepper, thinly sliced
- 1/2 cup sliced carrots
- 1/2 cup sliced mushrooms
- 1/2 cup coconut milk (lite version)
- 1 tbsp low-sodium soy sauce
- 1 tbsp curry powder
- 1 tsp minced garlic
- 1 tsp grated ginger
- 1 tbsp olive oil
- 2 cups cooked brown rice

Instructions:

1. In a bowl, combine the coconut milk, low-sodium soy sauce, curry powder, minced garlic, and grated ginger. Mix well and set aside.
2. In a large non-stick skillet or wok, heat the olive oil over medium-high heat.
3. Add the sliced carrots and cook for 2-3 minutes until they start to soften.
4. Add the broccoli, red bell pepper, and yellow bell pepper to the skillet. Stir-fry for another 2 minutes.
5. Add the sliced mushrooms and shrimp to the skillet. Cook for 3-4 minutes until the shrimp turn pink and are cooked through.
6. Pour the coconut milk mixture over the shrimp and vegetables in the skillet. Stir well to coat everything evenly. Cook for an additional 1-2 minutes until the sauce thickens slightly.
7. Divide the cooked brown rice between two plates.
8. Spoon the coconut curry shrimp stir-fry over the rice.
9. Serve hot and enjoy your heart-healthy and delicious Coconut Curry Shrimp Stir-Fry!

Nutritional Information (per serving):
Cal: 380 | Carbs: 33g | Pro: 24g | Fat: 17g | Chol: 145mg | Sod: 400mg | Fiber: 5g | Sugars: 6g

10. Cajun Blackened Catfish

Preparation time: 10 minutes
Servings: 2

Ingredients:

- 2 catfish fillets (about 6 ounces each)
- 1 tsp paprika
- 1/2 tsp garlic powder
- 1/2 tsp onion powder
- 1/2 tsp dried thyme
- 1/2 tsp dried oregano
- 1/4 tsp cayenne pepper (adjust to taste)
- 1/4 tsp black pepper
- 1/4 tsp salt
- Cooking spray

Instructions:

1. In a small bowl, mix paprika, garlic powder, onion powder, dried thyme, dried oregano, cayenne pepper, black pepper, and salt to create the Cajun seasoning.
2. Pat the catfish fillets dry with a paper towel and then coat them evenly with the Cajun seasoning on both sides.
3. Heat a non-stick skillet or grill pan over medium-high heat and coat it with cooking spray.
4. Once the pan is hot, add the seasoned catfish fillets and cook for about 3-4 minutes per side or until the fish is cooked through and has a blackened crust.
5. Remove the catfish from the pan and let it rest for a minute before serving.
6. Serve the Cajun Blackened Catfish with your favorite heart-healthy side dishes like steamed vegetables or a fresh green salad.

Nutritional Information (per serving):
Cal: 185 | Carbs: 1g | Pro: 29g | Fat: 6g | Chol: 80mg | Sod: 270mg | Fiber: 0g | Sugars: 0g

11. Mediterranean Stuffed Squid

Preparation time: 20 minutes
Servings: 4

Ingredients:

- 8 small to medium squid tubes
- 1 cup cooked quinoa
- 1/4 cup cherry tomatoes, diced
- 1/4 cup Kalamata olives, pitted and chopped
- 1/4 cup feta cheese, crumbled
- 2 tbsp fresh parsley, chopped
- 2 tbsp olive oil
- 2 cloves garlic, minced
- 1/4 tsp dried oregano
- 1/4 tsp black pepper
- 1 lemon, juiced
- Cooking spray

Instructions:

1. Preheat the oven to 375°F (190°C).
2. Clean the squid tubes thoroughly, removing any innards and rinsing them under cold water. Pat them dry with a paper towel.
3. In a large mixing bowl, combine the cooked quinoa, diced cherry tomatoes, chopped Kalamata olives, crumbled feta cheese, and fresh parsley.
4. In a separate small bowl, whisk together the olive oil, minced garlic, dried oregano, black pepper, and lemon juice.
5. Pour the olive oil mixture over the quinoa mixture and toss until well combined.
6. Stuff each squid tube with the quinoa mixture, leaving some space at the top to prevent overstuffing.

7. Secure the top of each squid tube with a toothpick to keep the filling in place.
8. Place the stuffed squid tubes in a baking dish coated with cooking spray.
9. Drizzle any remaining olive oil mixture over the stuffed squid.
10. Bake in the preheated oven for 15-18 minutes or until the squid is cooked through and tender.
11. Serve the Mediterranean Stuffed Squid with a fresh salad or whole-grain couscous.

Nutritional Information (per serving):
Cal: 220 | Carbs: 15g | Pro: 15g | Fat: 10g | Chol: 150mg | Sod: 260mg | Fiber: 2g | Sugars: 2g

12. Lime Cilantro Mahi Mahi

Preparation time: 10 minutes
Servings: 2

Ingredients:

- 2 Mahi-Mahi fillets (about 4-6 ounces each)
- 2 tablespoons fresh lime juice
- 2 tablespoons fresh cilantro, chopped
- 1 clove garlic, minced
- 1/4 teaspoon ground black pepper
- Cooking spray

Instructions:

1. Preheat the oven to 400°F (200°C).
2. Pat dry the Mahi-Mahi fillets with a paper towel and place them in a baking dish coated with cooking spray.
3. In a small bowl, mix the lime juice, chopped cilantro, minced garlic, and black pepper.
4. Pour the lime-cilantro mixture over the Mahi-Mahi fillets, ensuring they are evenly coated.
5. Cover the baking dish with aluminum foil and let the fish marinate in the refrigerator for 15-20 minutes.
6. Remove the dish from the refrigerator and uncover it.
7. Bake the Mahi-Mahi in the preheated oven for 12-15 minutes or until the fish is opaque and flakes easily with a fork.
8. Serve the Lime Cilantro Mahi-Mahi with your favorite heart-healthy sides, like steamed vegetables or a quinoa salad.

Nutritional Information (per serving):
Cal: 200 | Carbs: 2g | Pro: 36g | Fat: 3g | Chol: 150mg | Sod: 70mg | Fiber: 0g | Sugars: 0g

13. Steamed Ginger Soy Snapper

Preparation time: 15 minutes
Servings: 2

Ingredients:

- 2 snapper fillets (about 4-6 ounces each), skinless and boneless
- 1-inch piece of ginger, peeled and thinly sliced
- 2 tablespoons low-sodium soy sauce
- 1 tablespoon rice vinegar
- 1 tablespoon water
- 1 teaspoon sesame oil
- 1 clove garlic, minced
- 1 green onion, thinly sliced (for garnish)
- 1 tablespoon fresh cilantro, chopped (for garnish)
- 1 tablespoon toasted sesame seeds (for garnish)
- Cooking spray

Instructions:

1. Rinse the snapper fillets under cold water and pat them dry with paper towels. Set aside.
2. In a small bowl, mix the low-sodium soy sauce, rice vinegar, water, sesame oil, and minced garlic to create the marinade.
3. Place the snapper fillets in a shallow dish and pour the marinade over them, ensuring they are evenly coated. Add the thinly sliced ginger on top of the fillets. Cover the dish with plastic wrap and let it marinate in the refrigerator for 10 minutes.
4. While the fish is marinating, prepare your steamer. If you don't have a steamer, you can use a large saucepan or wok with a steamer basket. Add water to the bottom of the steamer or saucepan, making sure it doesn't touch the bottom of the basket.
5. Lightly coat the steamer or steamer basket with cooking spray to prevent sticking.
6. Place the marinated snapper fillets in the steamer or steamer basket. Discard the remaining marinade.
7. Steam the snapper over medium-high heat for about 6-8 minutes or until the fish is opaque and flakes easily with a fork.
8. Once the snapper is cooked, carefully remove it from the steamer and transfer it to serving plates.
9. Garnish the snapper with thinly sliced green onions, chopped cilantro, and toasted sesame seeds.
10. Serve the Steamed Ginger Soy Snapper hot and enjoy this heart-healthy and delicious dish!

Nutritional Information (per serving):
Cal: 170 | Carbs: 4g | Pro: 30g | Fat: 4g | Chol: 55mg | Sod: 320mg | Fiber: 1g | Sugars: 0g

14. Spicy Chipotle Fish Tacos

Preparation time: 15 minutes
Servings: 4

Ingredients:

- 1 lb white fish fillets (such as cod or tilapia)
- 2 tbsp olive oil
- 1 tbsp chipotle chili powder
- 1 tsp ground cumin
- 1/2 tsp garlic powder
- 1/2 tsp onion powder
- 1/4 tsp salt
- 8 small corn tortillas
- 1 cup shredded lettuce
- 1 cup diced tomatoes
- 1/2 cup diced red onion
- 1/4 cup chopped fresh cilantro
- Lime wedges, for serving

Instructions:

1. Preheat the oven to 400°F (200°C). Line a baking sheet with parchment paper or lightly grease it.
2. In a small bowl, mix together the chipotle chili powder, ground cumin, garlic powder, onion powder, and salt.
3. Pat the fish fillets dry with paper towels. Rub them with 1 tablespoon of olive oil and then sprinkle the chipotle spice mixture evenly over both sides of the fillets.
4. Place the seasoned fish on the prepared baking sheet and bake in the preheated oven for about 12-15 minutes or until the fish is cooked through and flakes easily with a fork.
5. While the fish is baking, warm the corn tortillas in a dry skillet over medium heat, about 1 minute per side, until they are soft and pliable.
6. To assemble the tacos, break the baked fish into smaller pieces. Lay a tortilla flat and add some shredded lettuce, diced tomatoes, red onion, and chopped cilantro. Top with a portion of the baked fish.
7. Drizzle a little of the remaining olive oil over the toppings and squeeze fresh lime juice on top.
8. Serve the Spicy Chipotle Fish Tacos with lime wedges on the side for an extra burst of flavor.

Nutritional Information (per serving):
Cal: 315 | Carbs: 22g | Pro: 23g | Fat: 14g | Chol: 50mg | Sod: 225mg | Fiber: 5g | Sugars: 4g

15. Herb Crusted Baked Haddock

Preparation time: 10 minutes
Servings: 4

Ingredients:

- 4 haddock fillets (about 4-6 ounces each)
- 1/4 cup whole wheat breadcrumbs
- 1/4 cup fresh parsley, chopped
- 2 tbsp grated Parmesan cheese
- 1 tbsp fresh lemon juice
- 1 tbsp olive oil
- 1/2 tsp garlic powder

- 1/2 tsp dried thyme
- 1/2 tsp dried oregano
- Cooking spray
- Lemon wedges (for serving)

Instructions:

1. Preheat the oven to 400°F (200°C). Line a baking sheet with parchment paper and lightly coat it with cooking spray.
2. In a shallow dish, mix together the whole wheat breadcrumbs, chopped parsley, grated Parmesan cheese, garlic powder, dried thyme, and dried oregano.
3. Drizzle the haddock fillets with fresh lemon juice and olive oil.
4. Press each haddock fillet into the breadcrumb mixture, ensuring it is evenly coated on both sides. Gently pat the breadcrumbs onto the fish.
5. Place the coated haddock fillets on the prepared baking sheet.
6. Bake in the preheated oven for 12-15 minutes or until the fish is cooked through and the crust is golden and crispy.
7. Serve the herb-crusted baked haddock with lemon wedges on the side.

Nutritional Information (per serving):
Cal: 220 | Carbs: 7g | Pro: 30g | Fat: 8g | Chol: 95mg | Sod: 260mg | Fiber: 1g | Sugars: 1g

16. Garlic Butter Scallops

Preparation time: 10 minutes
Servings: 2

Ingredients:

- 1/2 lb fresh scallops
- 2 tbsp unsalted butter
- 2 cloves garlic, minced
- 1 tbsp fresh lemon juice
- 1 tbsp fresh parsley, chopped
- Salt and pepper to taste
- Cooking spray

Instructions:

1. Pat dry the scallops using paper towels and season them with a pinch of salt and pepper.
2. In a non-stick skillet, melt 1 tablespoon of butter over medium-high heat and coat the pan with cooking spray.
3. Add the scallops to the skillet and sear them for about 2-3 minutes on each side until they turn golden brown and form a nice crust. Remove the scallops from the skillet and set them aside.
4. In the same skillet, melt the remaining tablespoon of butter over medium heat. Add the minced garlic and sauté for about 30 seconds until fragrant.

5. Add the fresh lemon juice to the skillet and stir to combine with the garlic butter.
6. Return the seared scallops to the skillet and toss them gently in the garlic butter sauce for about 1 minute to coat them evenly.
7. Sprinkle the chopped parsley over the scallops and give it a final toss.
8. Transfer the garlic butter scallops to a serving plate and enjoy them hot.

Nutritional Information (per serving):
Cal: 210 | Carbs: 3g | Pro: 17g | Fat: 13g | Chol: 50mg | Sod: 450mg | Fiber: 0g | Sugars: 0g

17. Teriyaki Glazed Swordfish

Preparation time: 10 minutes
Servings: 2

Ingredients:

- 2 swordfish steaks (about 6 oz each)
- 1/4 cup reduced-sodium soy sauce
- 2 tbsp honey
- 1 tbsp rice vinegar
- 1 clove garlic, minced
- 1/2 tsp grated fresh ginger
- 1/4 tsp black pepper
- 1 green onion, thinly sliced (for garnish)
- 1 tsp sesame seeds (for garnish)
- Cooking spray

Instructions:

1. In a small bowl, whisk together the reduced-sodium soy sauce, honey, rice vinegar, minced garlic, grated ginger, and black pepper to make the teriyaki glaze.
2. Place the swordfish steaks in a shallow dish and pour half of the teriyaki glaze over them, making sure to coat both sides. Reserve the remaining glaze for later.
3. Cover the dish with plastic wrap and marinate the swordfish in the refrigerator for at least 30 minutes.
4. Preheat your grill or grill pan over medium-high heat. Coat the grill grates with cooking spray to prevent sticking.
5. Remove the swordfish from the marinade and discard the marinade used for marinating.
6. Grill the swordfish steaks for about 4-5 minutes on each side or until they are cooked through and have nice grill marks.
7. While grilling, baste the swordfish with the reserved teriyaki glaze from time to time to enhance the flavor.
8. Once the swordfish is cooked, remove it from the grill and let it rest for a minute.
9. Serve the Teriyaki Glazed Swordfish garnished with sliced green onions and sesame seeds.

Nutritional Information (per serving):
Cal: 290 | Carbs: 17g | Pro: 33g | Fat: 10g | Chol: 90mg | Sod: 630mg | Fiber: 0.5g | Sugars: 15g

18. Pesto Grilled Sea Bass

Preparation time: 10 minutes
Servings: 2

Ingredients:

- 2 sea bass fillets (about 6 ounces each)
- 2 tablespoons low-sodium pesto sauce
- 1 tablespoon lemon juice
- 1/4 teaspoon black pepper
- Cooking spray

Instructions:

1. Preheat the grill to medium-high heat.
2. Pat the sea bass fillets dry with a paper towel.
3. In a small bowl, mix the pesto sauce and lemon juice together.
4. Brush both sides of the sea bass fillets with the pesto mixture.
5. Sprinkle black pepper evenly over the fillets.
6. Lightly coat the grill grates with cooking spray to prevent sticking.
7. Place the sea bass fillets on the grill and cook for about 4-5 minutes per side or until the fish is opaque and easily flakes with a fork.
8. Remove the grilled sea bass from the heat and serve hot.

Nutritional Information (per serving):
Cal: 220 | Carbs: 2g | Pro: 28g | Fat: 11g | Chol: 75mg | Sod: 150mg | Fiber: 0g | Sugars: 0g

19. Citrus Marinated Ceviche

Preparation time: 15 minutes
Servings: 4

Ingredients:

- 1 pound fresh white fish (such as tilapia or cod), deboned and diced
- 1 cup cherry tomatoes, halved
- 1/2 cup red onion, finely chopped
- 1/2 cup cucumber, diced
- 1/4 cup fresh cilantro, chopped
- 2 oranges, juiced
- 2 limes, juiced
- 1/4 tsp. ground cumin
- 1/4 tsp. chili powder
- Salt and pepper to taste
- Lettuce leaves, for serving (optional)

Instructions:

1. In a large mixing bowl, combine the diced white fish, cherry tomatoes, red onion, cucumber, and fresh cilantro.
2. In a separate small bowl, whisk together the freshly squeezed orange juice, lime juice, ground cumin, chili powder, salt, and pepper.
3. Pour the citrus marinade over the fish and vegetable mixture. Stir gently to ensure everything is coated with the marinade.
4. Cover the bowl with plastic wrap and refrigerate for at least 1 hour to allow the flavors to meld together. You can also refrigerate it overnight for a deeper flavor.
5. Before serving, taste the ceviche and adjust seasoning if needed.
6. Optionally, serve the citrus marinated ceviche on lettuce leaves for a fresh presentation.

Nutritional Information (per serving):
Cal: 150 | Carbs: 10g | Pro: 25g | Fat: 2g | Chol: 40mg | Sod: 100mg | Fiber: 2g | Sugars: 5g

20. Smoked Paprika Shrimp Salad

Preparation time: 15 minutes
Servings: 2

Ingredients:

- 8 oz (225g) cooked shrimp, peeled and deveined
- 2 cups mixed salad greens (e.g., spinach, arugula, lettuce)
- 1/2 cup cherry tomatoes, halved
- 1/4 cup cucumber, sliced
- 1/4 cup red bell pepper, sliced
- 2 tbsp fresh lemon juice
- 1 tbsp extra-virgin olive oil
- 1/2 tsp smoked paprika
- 1/4 tsp garlic powder
- Salt and pepper, to taste

Instructions:

1. In a large bowl, combine the cooked shrimp, mixed salad greens, cherry tomatoes, cucumber, and red bell pepper.
2. In a small bowl, whisk together the fresh lemon juice, extra-virgin olive oil, smoked paprika, garlic powder, salt, and pepper to make the dressing.
3. Pour the dressing over the shrimp and salad mixture. Toss gently to coat everything evenly.
4. Divide the smoked paprika shrimp salad into two serving plates or bowls.
5. Serve immediately and enjoy this heart-healthy and flavorful salad!

Nutritional Information (per serving):
Cal: 210 | Carbs: 8g | Pro: 22g | Fat: 10g | Chol: 150mg | Sod: 250mg | Fiber: 2g | Sugars: 3g

Vegetables and Grains

1. Lemon Herb Quinoa Salad

Preparation time: 15 minutes
Servings: 4

Ingredients:

- 1 cup quinoa, rinsed
- 2 cups water
- 1/4 cup fresh lemon juice
- 2 tbsp olive oil
- 1 tsp Dijon mustard
- 1 clove garlic, minced
- 1/4 cup fresh parsley, chopped
- 1/4 cup fresh mint leaves, chopped
- 1/4 cup fresh basil leaves, chopped
- 1/4 cup cherry tomatoes, halved
- 1/4 cup cucumber, diced
- 1/4 cup red bell pepper, diced
- Salt and pepper to taste

Instructions:

1. In a medium saucepan, bring the quinoa and water to a boil. Reduce heat to low, cover, and simmer for 12-15 minutes or until the quinoa is cooked and the water is absorbed. Fluff the quinoa with a fork and let it cool.
2. In a small bowl, whisk together the lemon juice, olive oil, Dijon mustard, minced garlic, salt, and pepper to make the dressing.
3. In a large mixing bowl, combine the cooked quinoa, chopped parsley, mint, and basil leaves.
4. Add the halved cherry tomatoes, diced cucumber, and diced red bell pepper to the bowl.
5. Pour the dressing over the quinoa and vegetables, and toss everything together until well coated.
6. Adjust salt and pepper to taste if needed.
7. Serve the Lemon Herb Quinoa Salad immediately, or refrigerate it for a few hours to let the flavors meld together before serving.

Nutritional Information (per serving):
Cal: 200 | Carbs: 30g | Pro: 5g | Fat: 7g | Chol: 0mg | Sod: 80mg | Fiber: 4g | Sugars: 2g

2. Roasted Veggie Buddha Bowl

Preparation time: 15 minutes
Servings: 2

Ingredients:

- 1 cup sweet potatoes, cubed
- 1 cup broccoli florets
- 1 cup cauliflower florets
- 1 cup chickpeas, cooked and drained
- 2 cups cooked quinoa
- 1 tablespoon olive oil
- 1/2 teaspoon garlic powder
- 1/2 teaspoon paprika
- 1/4 teaspoon salt
- 1/4 teaspoon black pepper
- 2 tablespoons hummus (optional, for serving)
- Fresh parsley or cilantro, for garnish

Instructions:

1. Preheat your oven to 425°F (220°C).
2. In a large mixing bowl, combine the sweet potatoes, broccoli, cauliflower, and chickpeas.
3. Drizzle olive oil over the vegetables and toss them to coat evenly.
4. Sprinkle garlic powder, paprika, salt, and black pepper over the vegetables and toss again to ensure they are well-seasoned.
5. Spread the seasoned vegetables and chickpeas on a baking sheet lined with parchment paper or a silicone baking mat.
6. Roast the vegetables in the preheated oven for about 15-20 minutes or until they are tender and lightly browned, tossing halfway through for even roasting.
7. While the vegetables are roasting, prepare the quinoa according to the package instructions if you haven't already.
8. Once the vegetables are done, divide the cooked quinoa and roasted veggies between two bowls.
9. If desired, add a dollop of hummus on top of each bowl for extra creaminess and flavor.
10. Garnish with fresh parsley or cilantro before serving.

Nutritional Information (per serving):
Cal: 480 | Carbs: 76g | Pro: 16g | Fat: 13g | Chol: 0mg | Sod: 320mg | Fiber: 15g | Sugars: 8g

3. Spicy Black Bean Tacos

Preparation time: 15 minutes
Servings: 4

Ingredients:

- 1 can (15 oz) low-sodium black beans, drained and rinsed
- 1 cup diced tomatoes
- 1/2 cup diced onions
- 1/2 cup diced bell peppers (any color)
- 2 cloves garlic, minced
- 1 tbsp olive oil
- 1 tsp ground cumin
- 1/2 tsp chili powder
- 1/4 tsp cayenne pepper (adjust to taste)
- Salt and pepper to taste
- 8 small corn tortillas
- Fresh cilantro, chopped (for garnish)
- Lime wedges (for serving)

Instructions:

1. In a medium-sized saucepan, heat the olive oil over medium heat. Add the minced garlic and sauté for about 1 minute until fragrant.
2. Add the diced onions and bell peppers to the saucepan. Cook for 2-3 minutes until they start to soften.
3. Stir in the black beans, diced tomatoes, ground cumin, chili powder, cayenne pepper, salt, and pepper. Cook the mixture for an additional 5 minutes, stirring occasionally, until everything is well combined and heated through.
4. While the bean mixture is cooking, warm the corn tortillas in a dry skillet over medium heat for about 30 seconds on each side.
5. To assemble the tacos, spoon the spicy black bean filling into the warm corn tortillas.
6. Garnish each taco with chopped cilantro.
7. Serve the Spicy Black Bean Tacos with lime wedges on the side for a burst of citrus flavor.

Nutritional Information (per serving):
Cal: 250 | Carbs: 38g | Pro: 9g | Fat: 7g | Chol: 0mg | Sod: 150mg | Fiber: 8g | Sugars: 4g

4. Mediterranean Stuffed Bell Peppers

Preparation time: 15 minutes
Servings: 4

Ingredients:

- 4 large bell peppers (any color), halved and seeds removed
- 1 cup cooked quinoa
- 1 can (15 oz) chickpeas, drained and rinsed
- 1 cup diced tomatoes (canned or fresh)
- 1/2 cup diced cucumber
- 1/4 cup chopped Kalamata olives
- 1/4 cup crumbled feta cheese (reduced-fat if available)
- 2 tablespoons chopped fresh parsley
- 1 tablespoon lemon juice
- 1 tablespoon extra-virgin olive oil
- 1 clove garlic, minced
- 1/2 teaspoon dried oregano
- Salt and pepper to taste

Instructions:

1. Preheat the oven to 375°F (190°C).
2. In a large mixing bowl, combine cooked quinoa, chickpeas, diced tomatoes, cucumber, Kalamata olives, feta cheese, chopped parsley, lemon juice, extra-virgin olive oil, minced garlic, dried oregano, salt, and pepper. Mix well until all the ingredients are evenly distributed.
3. Place the bell pepper halves on a baking sheet, cut side up.

4. Fill each bell pepper half with the Mediterranean mixture, pressing it down gently to pack it.
5. Cover the baking sheet with aluminum foil and bake in the preheated oven for 20-25 minutes or until the bell peppers are tender.
6. Remove the foil and bake for an additional 5 minutes to lightly brown the tops.
7. Once done, take the stuffed bell peppers out of the oven and let them cool slightly before serving.

Nutritional Information (per serving):
Cal: 290 | Carbs: 42g | Pro: 12g | Fat: 8g | Chol: 8mg | Sod: 540mg | Fiber: 9g | Sugars: 9g

5. Garlic Parmesan Cauliflower Rice

Preparation time: 10 minutes
Servings: 4

Ingredients:

- 1 medium head of cauliflower, riced (about 4 cups)
- 2 cloves garlic, minced
- 2 tablespoons olive oil
- 1/4 cup grated Parmesan cheese
- 1 tablespoon fresh parsley, chopped
- Salt and pepper to taste

Instructions:

1. Wash the cauliflower and remove the leaves and stem. Cut the cauliflower into florets.
2. Using a food processor, pulse the cauliflower florets until they resemble rice-like grains. You can also use a box grater or a knife to finely chop the cauliflower.
3. In a large skillet, heat the olive oil over medium heat. Add the minced garlic and sauté for about 1 minute until fragrant.
4. Add the cauliflower rice to the skillet and stir to combine with the garlic and oil. Cook for 3-4 minutes, stirring occasionally, until the cauliflower is tender but not mushy.
5. Stir in the grated Parmesan cheese and chopped parsley, and season with salt and pepper to taste.
6. Remove the skillet from the heat and transfer the garlic Parmesan cauliflower rice to a serving dish.

Nutritional Information (per serving):
Cal: 85 | Carbs: 7g | Pro: 3g | Fat: 5g | Chol: 3mg | Sod: 105mg | Fiber: 3g | Sugars: 3g

6. Spinach Lentil Curry

Preparation time: 10 minutes
Servings: 4

Ingredients:

- 1 cup dried red lentils
- 1 tbsp olive oil
- 1 large onion, finely chopped
- 3 cloves garlic, minced
- 1 tbsp grated fresh ginger
- 1 tsp ground cumin
- 1 tsp ground coriander
- 1/2 tsp ground turmeric
- 1/4 tsp cayenne pepper (optional, adjust to taste)
- 1 can (400g) diced tomatoes
- 3 cups fresh spinach leaves
- 1/2 cup lite coconut milk
- Salt and pepper to taste
- Fresh cilantro, for garnish (optional)
- Cooked brown rice or whole wheat naan, for serving (optional)

Instructions:

1. Rinse the dried red lentils in a fine-mesh strainer under cold running water until the water runs clear. Drain and set aside.
2. In a large pot or skillet, heat the olive oil over medium heat. Add the chopped onion and sauté for 2-3 minutes until softened.
3. Stir in the minced garlic and grated ginger, and cook for an additional minute until fragrant.
4. Add the ground cumin, ground coriander, ground turmeric, and cayenne pepper (if using). Cook the spices with the onions, garlic, and ginger for about 1 minute to release their flavors.
5. Add the rinsed lentils to the pot and stir well to coat them with the spice mixture.
6. Pour in the diced tomatoes (with their juice) and 1 cup of water. Stir everything together, then bring the mixture to a boil.
7. Reduce the heat to low, cover the pot, and let the curry simmer for 15-20 minutes, or until the lentils are tender and fully cooked.
8. Stir in the fresh spinach leaves and cook for another 2-3 minutes until the spinach wilts.
9. Pour in the lite coconut milk, and stir until everything is well combined. Cook for an additional 1-2 minutes to heat the coconut milk.
10. Season the spinach lentil curry with salt and pepper to taste.
11. Serve the curry hot over cooked brown rice or with whole wheat naan on the side. Garnish with fresh cilantro, if desired.

Nutritional Information (per serving):
Cal: 257 | Carbs: 37g | Pro: 14g | Fat: 6g | Chol: 0mg | Sod: 353mg | Fiber: 14g | Sugars: 7g

7. Balsamic Roasted Brussels Sprouts

Preparation time: 10 minutes
Servings: 4

Ingredients:

- 1 lb Brussels sprouts, trimmed and halved
- 2 tablespoons balsamic vinegar
- 1 tablespoon olive oil
- 1/2 teaspoon garlic powder
- 1/4 teaspoon salt (optional, for low sodium omit or reduce)
- 1/4 teaspoon black pepper

Instructions:

1. Preheat your oven to 400°F (200°C).
2. In a large mixing bowl, combine the halved Brussels sprouts, balsamic vinegar, olive oil, garlic powder, salt (if using), and black pepper. Toss until the Brussels sprouts are evenly coated with the mixture.
3. Spread the Brussels sprouts in a single layer on a baking sheet lined with parchment paper or lightly greased with cooking spray.
4. Roast the Brussels sprouts in the preheated oven for about 20-25 minutes or until they are tender and lightly browned, stirring once halfway through to ensure even roasting.
5. Remove from the oven and serve hot.

Nutritional Information (per serving):
Cal: 80 | Carbs: 10g | Pro: 4g | Fat: 3.5g | Chol: 0mg | Sod: 105mg | Fiber: 4g | Sugars: 2g

8. Herbed Brown Rice Pilaf

Preparation time: 10 minutes
Servings: 4

Ingredients:

- 1 cup brown rice
- 2 cups low-sodium vegetable broth
- 1/4 cup diced onions
- 1/4 cup diced carrots
- 1/4 cup diced celery
- 2 cloves garlic, minced
- 1/4 tsp dried thyme
- 1/4 tsp dried rosemary
- 1/4 tsp dried sage
- 1/4 tsp dried parsley
- 1 tbsp olive oil
- Salt and pepper to taste

Instructions:

1.
2. In a medium saucepan, heat olive oil over medium heat.
3. Add diced onions, carrots, and celery to the saucepan. Sauté for 2-3 minutes until slightly softened.
4. Add minced garlic to the vegetables and continue to sauté for another minute.
5. Add brown rice to the saucepan and stir to coat the rice with the vegetables and oil.

6. Pour in the low-sodium vegetable broth and bring to a boil.
7. Reduce the heat to low, cover the saucepan with a lid, and let the rice simmer for about 30 minutes or until the liquid is absorbed and the rice is tender.
8. Once the rice is cooked, fluff it with a fork and stir in the dried thyme, rosemary, sage, parsley, salt, and pepper.
9. Remove the saucepan from heat, cover it again, and let it sit for a few minutes to allow the flavors to meld.
10. Serve the herbed brown rice pilaf as a delicious and heart-healthy side dish or as a base for other dishes.

Nutritional Information (per serving):
Cal: 190 | Carbs: 34g | Pro: 4g | Fat: 4g | Chol: 0mg | Sod: 80mg | Fiber: 3g | Sugars: 2g

9. Zucchini Noodles Primavera

Preparation time: 15 minutes
Servings: 2

Ingredients:

- 2 medium zucchinis
- 1 cup cherry tomatoes, halved
- 1/2 cup sliced bell peppers (any color)
- 1/4 cup diced red onion
- 2 cloves garlic, minced
- 1/4 tsp. dried basil
- 1/4 tsp. dried oregano
- 1/4 tsp. crushed red pepper flakes (optional, for a spicy kick)
- 1 tbsp. olive oil
- Salt and pepper to taste
- Fresh basil leaves, for garnish
- Grated Parmesan cheese, for serving (optional)

Instructions:

1. Using a spiralizer or vegetable peeler, create zucchini noodles (zoodles) from the zucchinis. Set aside.
2. In a large non-stick skillet, heat the olive oil over medium heat.
3. Add the minced garlic and sauté for about 30 seconds until fragrant.
4. Add the diced red onion and sliced bell peppers to the skillet. Sauté for 2-3 minutes until the vegetables start to soften.
5. Toss in the halved cherry tomatoes, dried basil, dried oregano, and crushed red pepper flakes (if using). Cook for an additional 2 minutes until the tomatoes begin to release their juices.
6. Add the zucchini noodles to the skillet and gently toss with the sautéed vegetables until everything is well combined. Cook for 2-3 minutes until the

zucchini noodles are just tender but still slightly crisp.
7. Season with salt and pepper according to your taste preferences.
8. Divide the Zucchini Noodles Primavera into two servings, and garnish each portion with fresh basil leaves.
9. If desired, serve with a sprinkle of grated Parmesan cheese on top.

Nutritional Information (per serving):
Cal: 130 | Carbs: 12g | Pro: 4g | Fat: 8g | Chol: 0mg | Sod: 15mg | Fiber: 4g | Sugars: 8g

10. Chickpea Avocado Salad

Preparation time: 15 minutes
Servings: 4

Ingredients:

- 1 can (15 oz) chickpeas, drained and rinsed
- 1 large avocado, diced
- 1 cup cherry tomatoes, halved
- 1/4 cup red onion, finely chopped
- 1/4 cup fresh cilantro, chopped
- 2 tablespoons lime juice
- 1 tablespoon extra-virgin olive oil
- Salt and pepper to taste

Instructions:

1. In a large mixing bowl, combine the chickpeas, diced avocado, halved cherry tomatoes, chopped red onion, and fresh cilantro.
2. Drizzle the lime juice and extra-virgin olive oil over the salad ingredients.
3. Gently toss all the ingredients together until well combined.
4. Season with salt and pepper to taste.
5. Serve the Chickpea Avocado Salad immediately or refrigerate for 30 minutes to allow the flavors to meld.

Nutritional Information (per serving):
Cal: 215 | Carbs: 22g | Pro: 7g | Fat: 12g | Chol: 0mg | Sod: 150mg | Fiber: 9g | Sugars: 2g

11. Turmeric Spiced Couscous

Preparation time: 10 minutes
Servings: 4

Ingredients:

- 1 cup couscous
- 1 3/4 cups low-sodium vegetable broth
- 1/2 tsp ground turmeric
- 1/4 tsp ground cumin

- 1/4 tsp ground coriander
- 1/4 tsp ground ginger
- 1/4 tsp salt (optional)
- 1/4 cup chopped fresh parsley
- 1/4 cup chopped fresh mint
- 1/4 cup chopped cucumber
- 1/4 cup diced red bell pepper
- 1/4 cup diced red onion
- 1/4 cup sliced black olives
- 2 tbsp lemon juice
- 1 tbsp olive oil

Instructions:

1. In a medium saucepan, bring the low-sodium vegetable broth to a boil. Stir in the ground turmeric, ground cumin, ground coriander, ground ginger, and optional salt.
2. Remove the saucepan from heat and stir in the couscous. Cover the saucepan with a lid and let it sit for 5 minutes.
3. Fluff the couscous with a fork and transfer it to a large mixing bowl.
4. In the mixing bowl with couscous, add chopped fresh parsley, chopped fresh mint, diced cucumber, diced red bell pepper, diced red onion, and sliced black olives. Toss the ingredients together.
5. In a small bowl, whisk together lemon juice and olive oil to make the dressing.
6. Pour the dressing over the couscous mixture and toss until everything is well combined.
7. Serve the Turmeric Spiced Couscous warm or at room temperature.

Nutritional Information (per serving):
Cal: 230 | Carbs: 38g | Pro: 5g | Fat: 7g | Chol: 0mg | Sod: 160mg | Fiber: 4g | Sugars: 2g

12. Ratatouille Stuffed Eggplant

Preparation time: 15 minutes
Servings: 4

Ingredients:

- 2 medium-sized eggplants
- 1 zucchini, diced
- 1 yellow squash, diced
- 1 red bell pepper, diced
- 1 yellow bell pepper, diced
- 1 small onion, diced
- 3 cloves garlic, minced
- 1 can (14 oz) diced tomatoes, no salt added
- 1 tbsp olive oil
- 1 tsp dried basil
- 1 tsp dried thyme
- 1/2 tsp dried oregano
- Salt and pepper to taste
- Fresh basil leaves, for garnish

Instructions:

1. Preheat the oven to 375°F (190°C).
2. Cut the eggplants in half lengthwise, and scoop out the centers, leaving about a 1/2-inch thick shell. Reserve the scooped-out eggplant flesh.
3. In a large skillet, heat olive oil over medium heat. Add the diced onion and minced garlic, and sauté until the onions become translucent.
4. Add the diced zucchini, yellow squash, red bell pepper, and yellow bell pepper to the skillet. Sauté for 5-7 minutes until the vegetables are slightly tender.
5. Stir in the reserved scooped-out eggplant flesh and canned diced tomatoes. Add dried basil, dried thyme, dried oregano, salt, and pepper. Mix well and cook for an additional 5 minutes.
6. Stuff the hollowed eggplant shells with the ratatouille mixture, pressing down gently to fit in as much as possible.
7. Place the stuffed eggplants in a baking dish and cover with foil. Bake in the preheated oven for 25-30 minutes or until the eggplants are tender.
8. Remove the foil and bake for an additional 5 minutes to lightly brown the top.
9. Garnish with fresh basil leaves before serving.

Nutritional Information (per serving):
Cal: 180 | Carbs: 30g | Pro: 5g | Fat: 6g | Chol: 0mg | Sod: 20mg | Fiber: 12g | Sugars: 14g

13. Cilantro Lime Brown Rice

Preparation time: 5 minutes
Servings: 4

Ingredients:

- 1 cup brown rice
- 2 cups water
- 1/4 cup fresh cilantro, chopped
- 1 lime, juiced
- 1/4 tsp. salt (optional)
- Cooking spray

Instructions:

1. In a fine-mesh strainer, rinse the brown rice thoroughly under cold water.
2. In a medium saucepan, bring the 2 cups of water to a boil. Add the rinsed brown rice and a pinch of salt (if desired).
3. Reduce the heat to low, cover the saucepan with a lid, and simmer for 40-45 minutes or until the rice is tender and cooked.
4. Once the rice is cooked, fluff it with a fork and let it cool for a few minutes.
5. In a separate bowl, combine the chopped cilantro and lime juice.
6. Add the cilantro lime mixture to the cooked

brown rice and gently toss until well combined.
7. Serve the Cilantro Lime Brown Rice as a delicious and heart-healthy side dish.

Nutritional Information (per serving):
Cal: 180 | Carbs: 38g | Pro: 4g | Fat: 1g | Chol: 0mg | Sod: 150mg | Fiber: 2g | Sugars: 0g

14. Caprese Quinoa Skewers

Preparation time: 20 minutes
Servings: 4

Ingredients:

- 1 cup quinoa, rinsed
- 2 cups cherry tomatoes
- 1 cup fresh mozzarella balls (bocconcini)
- Fresh basil leaves
- Balsamic glaze (store-bought or homemade)
- Salt and pepper to taste
- Wooden skewers

Instructions:

1. Cook the quinoa according to the package instructions. Once cooked, let it cool to room temperature.
2. Assemble the skewers by threading the ingredients onto the wooden skewers in the following order: cherry tomato, cooked quinoa, fresh mozzarella ball, and fresh basil leaf. Repeat until each skewer is filled, making sure to leave a little space at the end for easy handling.
3. Arrange the Caprese Quinoa Skewers on a serving platter.
4. Drizzle the balsamic glaze over the skewers.
5. Season the skewers with salt and pepper to taste.
6. Serve and enjoy these delightful Caprese Quinoa Skewers as a heart-healthy and delicious appetizer or light meal.

Nutritional Information (per serving):
Cal: 270 | Carbs: 32g | Pro: 12g | Fat: 11g | Chol: 20mg | Sod: 120mg | Fiber: 4g | Sugars: 3g

15. Grilled Portobello Mushrooms

Preparation time: 10 minutes
Servings: 2

Ingredients:

- 2 large Portobello mushrooms
- 2 tbsp balsamic vinegar
- 2 tbsp low-sodium soy sauce
- 2 cloves garlic, minced
- 1 tbsp olive oil
- 1/4 tsp black pepper
- Cooking spray

Instructions:

1. Clean the Portobello mushrooms by gently wiping them with a damp paper towel. Remove the stems and scrape out the gills with a spoon to create more room for the marinade.
2. In a shallow dish, mix balsamic vinegar, low-sodium soy sauce, minced garlic, olive oil, and black pepper to make the marinade.
3. Place the mushrooms in the marinade, turning them to coat both sides. Let them marinate for about 10 minutes, allowing the flavors to infuse.
4. Preheat the grill or grill pan over medium heat. Lightly coat the grill grates with cooking spray to prevent sticking.
5. Place the marinated Portobello mushrooms on the grill, cap side down. Grill for about 5-6 minutes on each side, or until tender, basting occasionally with the remaining marinade.
6. Once the mushrooms are cooked to your liking, remove them from the grill.
7. Serve the grilled Portobello mushrooms as a delicious and heart-healthy main dish or as a tasty addition to salads and sandwiches.

Nutritional Information (per serving):
Cal: 60 | Carbs: 6g | Pro: 3g | Fat: 4g | Chol: 0mg | Sod: 220mg | Fiber: 2g | Sugars: 3g

16. Greek Orzo Salad

Preparation time: 15 minutes
Servings: 4

Ingredients:

- 1 cup whole wheat orzo pasta
- 1 cup cherry tomatoes, halved
- 1 cucumber, diced
- 1/4 cup red onion, finely chopped
- 1/4 cup Kalamata olives, pitted and sliced
- 1/4 cup crumbled feta cheese
- 2 tablespoons fresh parsley, chopped
- 2 tablespoons fresh lemon juice
- 1 tablespoon extra-virgin olive oil
- 1 teaspoon dried oregano
- Salt and pepper to taste

Instructions:

1. Cook the whole wheat orzo pasta according to the package instructions. Drain and rinse with cold water to cool.
2. In a large mixing bowl, combine the cooked orzo, cherry tomatoes, cucumber, red onion, Kalamata olives, and crumbled feta cheese.
3. In a small bowl, whisk together the fresh lemon juice, extra-virgin olive oil, dried oregano, salt, and pepper.
4. Pour the dressing over the salad and toss

everything together until well combined.

5. Sprinkle the chopped parsley on top and give the salad a final toss.
6. Serve the Greek Orzo Salad immediately or refrigerate for a few hours to let the flavors meld together.

Nutritional Information (per serving):
Cal: 270 | Carbs: 32g | Pro: 12g | Fat: 11g | Chol: 20mg | Sod: 120mg | Fiber: 4g | Sugars: 3g

17. Asparagus Lemon Risotto

Preparation time: 10 minutes
Servings: 4

Ingredients:

• 1 cup Arborio rice
• 4 cups low-sodium vegetable broth
• 1 cup fresh asparagus, trimmed and cut into bite-sized pieces
• 1 small onion, finely chopped
• 2 cloves garlic, minced
• 1 lemon, zest and juice
• 2 tbsp olive oil
• 1/4 cup grated Parmesan cheese
• Salt and pepper to taste
• Fresh parsley, chopped (for garnish)

Instructions:

1. In a medium-sized saucepan, heat the vegetable broth over low heat. Keep it warm but not boiling.
2. In a separate large saucepan or deep skillet, heat the olive oil over medium heat. Add the chopped onion and sauté until it becomes translucent, about 2-3 minutes.
3. Add the minced garlic to the pan and cook for another minute, stirring frequently.
4. Stir in the Arborio rice and cook for 1-2 minutes, allowing it to toast slightly.
5. Gradually add the warm vegetable broth to the rice, one ladleful at a time, stirring constantly. Allow the liquid to be absorbed by the rice before adding the next ladleful. Continue this process until the rice is creamy and cooked to al dente, which should take about 18-20 minutes.
6. During the last 5 minutes of cooking, add the chopped asparagus to the risotto and stir it in gently.
7. Once the risotto and asparagus are cooked, remove the pan from the heat. Stir in the lemon zest, lemon juice, and grated Parmesan cheese. Season with salt and pepper to taste.
8. Serve the Asparagus Lemon Risotto in individual plates or bowls. Garnish with chopped fresh parsley for added flavor and presentation.

Nutritional Information (per serving):
Cal: 275 | Carbs: 44g | Pro: 7g | Fat: 8g | Chol: 6mg | Sod: 210mg | Fiber: 3g | Sugars: 2g

18. Sweet Potato Kale Hash

Preparation time: 15 minutes
Servings: 2

Ingredients:

• 2 cups sweet potatoes, peeled and diced
• 2 cups kale, chopped
• 1/2 cup red bell pepper, diced
• 1/4 cup red onion, diced
• 1 clove garlic, minced
• 1/2 tsp. smoked paprika
• 1/4 tsp. ground black pepper
• 1/4 tsp. salt (optional)
• 1 tbsp. olive oil

Instructions:

1. Heat the olive oil in a large skillet over medium heat.
2. Add the diced sweet potatoes to the skillet and cook for 5 minutes, stirring occasionally, until they start to soften.
3. Add the diced red bell pepper, red onion, and minced garlic to the skillet. Continue to cook for another 3-4 minutes until the vegetables are tender.
4. Stir in the chopped kale, smoked paprika, ground black pepper, and salt (if using). Cook for an additional 2-3 minutes until the kale wilts.
5. Once the vegetables are cooked to your desired tenderness, remove the skillet from heat.
6. Serve the Sweet Potato Kale Hash hot as a delicious and heart-healthy side dish or a light meal.

Nutritional Information (per serving):
Cal: 215 | Carbs: 31g | Pro: 4g | Fat: 9g | Chol: 0mg | Sod: 95mg | Fiber: 6g | Sugars: 6g

19. Quinoa Spinach Stuffed Tomatoes

Preparation time: 15 minutes
Servings: 4

Ingredients:

• 4 large tomatoes
• 1 cup cooked quinoa
• 1 cup fresh spinach, chopped
• 1/4 cup red onion, finely chopped
• 1/4 cup crumbled feta cheese
• 1/4 cup fresh parsley, chopped
• 1 tbsp olive oil
• 1 garlic clove, minced

- 1/2 tsp dried oregano
- Salt and pepper to taste

Instructions:

1. Preheat the oven to 375°F (190°C).
2. Cut the tops off the tomatoes and carefully scoop out the seeds and pulp using a spoon. Be gentle not to puncture the tomatoes. Set aside.
3. In a large mixing bowl, combine the cooked quinoa, chopped spinach, red onion, feta cheese, parsley, olive oil, minced garlic, dried oregano, salt, and pepper. Mix well until all the ingredients are evenly distributed.
4. Stuff each tomato with the quinoa-spinach mixture, pressing it gently to fill the tomatoes.
5. Place the stuffed tomatoes in a baking dish and bake in the preheated oven for 20-25 minutes or until the tomatoes are slightly softened, and the filling is heated through.

Nutritional Information (per serving):
Cal: 170 | Carbs: 23g | Pro: 6g | Fat: 6g | Chol: 8mg | Sod: 110mg | Fiber: 5g | Sugars: 6g

20. Roasted Garlic Cauliflower Mash

Preparation time: 10 minutes
Servings: 4

Ingredients:

- 1 medium head cauliflower, cut into florets
- 1 tablespoon olive oil
- 3 cloves garlic, peeled
- 1/4 cup low-sodium vegetable broth
- 1/4 cup plain Greek yogurt
- Salt and pepper to taste
- Fresh chives (optional, for garnish)

Instructions:

1. Preheat the oven to 400°F (200°C).
2. In a large mixing bowl, toss the cauliflower florets with olive oil until they are evenly coated.
3. Place the cauliflower and garlic cloves on a baking sheet lined with parchment paper or a silicone mat.
4. Roast the cauliflower and garlic in the preheated oven for 20-25 minutes or until the cauliflower is tender and slightly browned.
5. In a blender or food processor, combine the roasted cauliflower, roasted garlic, low-sodium vegetable broth, and plain Greek yogurt. Blend until smooth and creamy.
6. Season the cauliflower mash with salt and pepper to taste.
7. Transfer the cauliflower mash to a serving dish and garnish with fresh chives, if desired.
8. Serve the roasted garlic cauliflower mash hot as a

delicious and heart-healthy side dish.

Nutritional Information (per serving):
Cal: 70 | Carbs: 8g | Pro: 4g | Fat: 3.5g | Chol: 0mg | Sod: 50mg | Fiber: 3g | Sugars: 3g

Salads

1. Citrus Avocado Delight

Preparation time: 10 minutes
Servings: 2

Ingredients:

- 1 large ripe avocado, diced
- 1 medium orange, peeled and segmented
- 1 medium grapefruit, peeled and segmented
- 1 tbsp fresh lime juice
- 1 tbsp fresh lemon juice
- 1 tbsp honey or maple syrup (optional, for sweetness)
- Fresh mint leaves for garnish (optional)

Instructions:

1. In a medium bowl, combine the diced avocado, orange segments, and grapefruit segments.
2. In a small bowl, whisk together the fresh lime juice, fresh lemon juice, and optional honey or maple syrup for added sweetness.
3. Pour the citrus dressing over the avocado and fruit mixture. Gently toss to coat all the ingredients evenly.
4. Divide the Citrus Avocado Delight into serving bowls or plates.
5. Garnish with fresh mint leaves if desired.
6. Serve immediately and enjoy this heart-healthy and refreshing dessert!

Nutritional Information (per serving):
Cal: 150 | Carbs: 18g | Pro: 2g | Fat: 9g | Chol: 0mg | Sod: 5mg | Fiber: 6g | Sugars: 9g

2. Spinach Berry Medley

Preparation time: 5 minutes
Servings: 2

Ingredients:

- 2 cups fresh spinach leaves
- 1 cup mixed berries (e.g., strawberries, blueberries, raspberries)
- 1 tablespoon chopped almonds (optional)
- 1 tablespoon balsamic vinegar
- 1 teaspoon honey
- 1/4 teaspoon ground cinnamon

Instructions:

1. In a large bowl, combine the fresh spinach leaves and mixed berries.
2. If desired, sprinkle the chopped almonds over the top for added crunch and flavor.
3. Drizzle the balsamic vinegar and honey over the salad.
4. Sprinkle the ground cinnamon on top for a touch of warmth and sweetness.
5. Gently toss all the ingredients together until the spinach and berries are evenly coated with the dressing.
6. Serve immediately and enjoy the refreshing and heart-healthy Spinach Berry Medley.

Nutritional Information (per serving):
Cal: 85 | Carbs: 12g | Pro: 2g | Fat: 3g | Chol: 0mg | Sod: 15mg | Fiber: 4g | Sugars: 7g

3. Quinoa Veggie Mix

Preparation time: 15 minutes
Servings: 4

Ingredients:

- 1 cup quinoa, rinsed and drained
- 2 cups water
- 1 cup cherry tomatoes, halved
- 1 cup cucumber, diced
- 1/2 cup red bell pepper, diced
- 1/4 cup red onion, finely chopped
- 1/4 cup fresh parsley, chopped
- 2 tbsp lemon juice
- 1 tbsp olive oil
- 1/2 tsp salt (optional)
- 1/4 tsp black pepper
- 1/4 tsp garlic powder

Instructions:

1. In a medium saucepan, combine the quinoa and water. Bring to a boil, then reduce the heat to low, cover, and simmer for 12-15 minutes or until the quinoa is cooked and the water is absorbed. Fluff with a fork and let it cool.
2. In a large mixing bowl, add the cooked quinoa, halved cherry tomatoes, diced cucumber, diced red bell pepper, finely chopped red onion, and chopped fresh parsley.
3. In a small bowl, whisk together the lemon juice, olive oil, salt (if using), black pepper, and garlic powder to make the dressing.
4. Pour the dressing over the quinoa and vegetable mixture, and toss everything together until well combined.
5. Serve the Quinoa Veggie Mix as a refreshing salad or a side dish.

Nutritional Information (per serving):
Cal: 225 | Carbs: 35g | Pro: 6g | Fat: 7g | Chol: 0mg | Sod: 150mg | Fiber: 5g | Sugars: 4g

4. Mediterranean Power Bowl

Preparation time: 15 minutes
Servings: 2

Ingredients:

- 1 cup cooked quinoa
- 1 cup canned chickpeas, drained and rinsed
- 1 cup cherry tomatoes, halved
- 1 cup cucumber, diced
- 1/4 cup Kalamata olives, pitted and sliced
- 1/4 cup red onion, finely chopped
- 2 tablespoons crumbled feta cheese
- 2 tablespoons fresh parsley, chopped
- 2 tablespoons lemon juice
- 2 tablespoons extra-virgin olive oil
- 1/2 teaspoon dried oregano
- Salt and pepper to taste

Instructions:

1. In a large mixing bowl, combine the cooked quinoa, chickpeas, cherry tomatoes, cucumber, Kalamata olives, and red onion.
2. In a small bowl, whisk together the lemon juice, extra-virgin olive oil, dried oregano, salt, and pepper to make the dressing.
3. Drizzle the dressing over the quinoa mixture and toss gently to coat all the ingredients.
4. Divide the Mediterranean Power Bowl into two serving bowls.
5. Sprinkle each bowl with crumbled feta cheese and chopped fresh parsley.
6. Serve immediately and enjoy this heart-healthy Mediterranean delight!

Nutritional Information (per serving):
Cal: 405 | Carbs: 52g | Pro: 14g | Fat: 18g | Chol: 8mg | Sod: 399mg | Fiber: 11g | Sugars: 6g

5. Zesty Tuna Crunch

Preparation time: 10 minutes
Servings: 2

Ingredients:

- 1 can (5 oz) tuna, packed in water, drained
- 1/4 cup celery, finely diced
- 1/4 cup red bell pepper, finely diced
- 2 tbsp light mayonnaise
- 1 tsp Dijon mustard
- 1/2 tsp lemon juice
- 1/4 tsp black pepper
- 2 cups mixed salad greens
- 1/4 cup cucumber, sliced
- 1/4 cup cherry tomatoes, halved
- 1/4 cup shredded carrots
- 1/4 cup whole-grain croutons (optional for added crunch)

Instructions:

1. In a medium-sized bowl, combine the drained tuna, diced celery, diced red bell pepper, light

mayonnaise, Dijon mustard, lemon juice, and black pepper. Mix well until all ingredients are evenly coated.
2. In a separate large bowl, toss together the mixed salad greens, cucumber slices, cherry tomatoes, and shredded carrots.
3. Divide the tuna mixture equally and place it on top of the salad mixture in the large bowl.
4. Gently toss the salad and tuna together until they are well combined.
5. If desired, sprinkle whole-grain croutons on top of the salad for extra crunch and texture.
6. Serve the Zesty Tuna Crunch salad immediately and enjoy the heart-healthy goodness!

Nutritional Information (per serving):
Cal: 210 | Carbs: 10g | Pro: 19g | Fat: 10g | Chol: 25mg | Sod: 370mg | Fiber: 3g | Sugars: 5g

6. Cucumber Dill Bliss

Preparation time: 10 minutes
Servings: 2

Ingredients:

- 2 medium cucumbers, thinly sliced
- 1/4 cup plain low-fat yogurt
- 1 tbsp fresh dill, chopped
- 1 tbsp fresh lemon juice
- 1/4 tsp garlic powder
- 1/4 tsp black pepper
- 1/8 tsp salt (optional)

Instructions:

1. In a medium bowl, combine the thinly sliced cucumbers, plain low-fat yogurt, fresh dill, and fresh lemon juice.
2. Sprinkle garlic powder and black pepper over the cucumber mixture.
3. If desired, add a pinch of salt for extra flavor (remember, a heart-healthy diet encourages reducing sodium, so use it sparingly or omit it).
4. Toss all the ingredients together until the cucumbers are well coated with the yogurt dressing.
5. Refrigerate the Cucumber Dill Bliss for at least 15 minutes to allow the flavors to meld.
6. Serve chilled as a refreshing and heart-healthy side dish or a light snack.

Nutritional Information (per serving):
Cal: 30 | Carbs: 5g | Pro: 2g | Fat: 0g | Chol: 1mg | Sod: 30mg | Fiber: 1g | Sugars: 3g

7. Beetroot Apple Slaw

Preparation time: 15 minutes
Servings: 4

Ingredients:

- 2 medium beetroots, peeled and grated
- 2 apples, cored and grated
- 1/4 cup chopped fresh cilantro (coriander)
- 1/4 cup chopped walnuts
- 2 tablespoons apple cider vinegar
- 1 tablespoon honey
- 1 tablespoon extra-virgin olive oil
- 1/4 teaspoon salt
- 1/4 teaspoon black pepper

Instructions:

1. In a large mixing bowl, combine the grated beetroots, grated apples, chopped cilantro, and chopped walnuts.
2. In a separate small bowl, whisk together the apple cider vinegar, honey, olive oil, salt, and black pepper to make the dressing.
3. Pour the dressing over the beetroot and apple mixture. Toss everything together until well combined and evenly coated.
4. Let the slaw sit for a few minutes to allow the flavors to meld together.
5. Serve the Beetroot Apple Slaw as a refreshing and heart-healthy side dish or a light meal.

Nutritional Information (per serving):
Cal: 120 | Carbs: 18g | Pro: 2g | Fat: 5g | Chol: 0mg | Sod: 130mg | Fiber: 4g | Sugars: 13g

8. Grilled Peach Arugula

Preparation time: 10 minutes
Servings: 2

Ingredients:

- 2 ripe peaches, halved and pitted
- 2 cups arugula
- 1/4 cup crumbled feta cheese
- 2 tablespoons balsamic vinegar
- 1 tablespoon extra-virgin olive oil
- 1/4 teaspoon black pepper

Instructions:

1. Preheat the grill or grill pan over medium-high heat.
2. Lightly brush the peach halves with olive oil to prevent sticking.
3. Place the peaches on the grill, cut side down, and cook for 3-4 minutes until grill marks appear and the peaches soften slightly.
4. Meanwhile, in a small bowl, whisk together the balsamic vinegar, extra-virgin olive oil, and black pepper to make the dressing.
5. Once the peaches are grilled, remove them from the grill and let them cool slightly.

In a large bowl, add the arugula and drizzle half of the dressing over it. Toss gently to coat the arugula.
6. Divide the dressed arugula between two plates.
7. Place the grilled peach halves on top of the arugula.
8. Sprinkle crumbled feta cheese over the salad.
9. Drizzle the remaining dressing over the peaches.
10. Serve the Grilled Peach Arugula salad immediately and enjoy!

Nutritional Information (per serving):
Cal: 125 | Carbs: 14g | Pro: 3g | Fat: 7g | Chol: 8mg | Sod: 94mg | Fiber: 2g | Sugars: 11g

9. Broccoli Almond Crunch

Preparation time: 15 minutes
Servings: 4

Ingredients:

- 4 cups fresh broccoli florets
- 1/4 cup sliced almonds
- 1 tbsp olive oil
- 1 tbsp lemon juice
- 1/4 tsp garlic powder
- 1/4 tsp onion powder
- 1/4 tsp salt (optional, to taste)
- 1/4 tsp black pepper

Instructions:

1. Preheat the oven to 400°F (200°C) and line a baking sheet with parchment paper.
2. In a large bowl, toss the broccoli florets with olive oil, lemon juice, garlic powder, onion powder, salt (if using), and black pepper until the broccoli is evenly coated.
3. Spread the seasoned broccoli on the prepared baking sheet in a single layer.
4. Sprinkle the sliced almonds over the broccoli.
5. Bake in the preheated oven for 12-15 minutes or until the broccoli is tender and the almonds are toasted and lightly browned.
6. Remove from the oven and let it cool for a minute before serving.

Nutritional Information (per serving):
Cal: 80 | Carbs: 6g | Pro: 3g | Fat: 6g | Chol: 0mg | Sod: 75mg | Fiber: 3g | Sugars: 1g

10. Fiesta Black Bean Salad

Preparation time: 15 minutes
Servings: 4

Ingredients:

- 1 can (15 oz) black beans, drained and rinsed
- 1 cup corn kernels (fresh, frozen, or canned)
- 1 cup cherry tomatoes, halved
- 1/2 cup diced bell peppers (any color)
- 1/4 cup diced red onion
- 1 jalapeño pepper, finely chopped (seeds removed for less heat)
- 1/4 cup chopped fresh cilantro
- 2 tablespoons fresh lime juice
- 1 tablespoon olive oil
- 1/4 teaspoon ground cumin
- Salt and pepper to taste

Instructions:

1. In a large mixing bowl, combine the black beans, corn, cherry tomatoes, bell peppers, red onion, jalapeño, and fresh cilantro.
2. In a small bowl, whisk together the fresh lime juice, olive oil, ground cumin, salt, and pepper to make the dressing.
3. Pour the dressing over the bean and vegetable mixture and toss everything together until well combined.
4. Adjust the seasoning to taste, adding more salt, pepper, or lime juice if desired.
5. Cover the bowl with plastic wrap or a lid and refrigerate the salad for at least 30 minutes to allow the flavors to meld.
6. Serve the Fiesta Black Bean Salad chilled, garnished with additional cilantro if desired.

Nutritional Information (per serving):
Cal: 150 | Carbs: 26g | Pro: 7g | Fat: 3g | Chol: 0mg | Sod: 180mg | Fiber: 7g | Sugars: 3g

11. Watermelon Feta Refresh

Preparation time: 10 minutes
Servings: 4

Ingredients:

- 4 cups cubed watermelon
- 1/2 cup crumbled feta cheese
- 1/4 cup fresh mint leaves, chopped
- 1 tablespoon balsamic glaze (optional)

Instructions:

1. In a large mixing bowl, combine the cubed watermelon, crumbled feta cheese, and chopped fresh mint.
2. Gently toss the ingredients together until the watermelon is evenly coated with the feta and mint.
3. Drizzle the balsamic glaze over the watermelon salad for an extra burst of flavor (optional).
4. Serve the Watermelon Feta Refresh immediately or refrigerate for a refreshing and chilled summer treat.

Nutritional Information (per serving):
Cal: 95 | Carbs: 15g | Pro: 3g | Fat: 3g | Chol: 11mg | Sod: 174mg | Fiber: 1g | Sugars: 12g

12. Asian Edamame Crunch

Preparation time: 10 minutes
Servings: 4

Ingredients:

- 2 cups frozen edamame, shelled
- 1 cup shredded carrots
- 1 cup red cabbage, thinly sliced
- 1/4 cup sliced almonds
- 2 green onions, thinly sliced
- 2 tbsp low-sodium soy sauce
- 1 tbsp rice vinegar
- 1 tbsp honey
- 1 tsp sesame oil
- 1/4 tsp ground ginger
- 1/4 tsp crushed red pepper flakes (optional)

Instructions:

1. In a large bowl, combine the frozen edamame, shredded carrots, red cabbage, sliced almonds, and green onions.
2. In a separate small bowl, whisk together the low-sodium soy sauce, rice vinegar, honey, sesame oil, ground ginger, and crushed red pepper flakes (if using) to make the dressing.
3. Pour the dressing over the edamame mixture and toss everything together until well coated.
4. Serve immediately or refrigerate for later.

Nutritional Information (per serving):
Cal: 180 | Carbs: 16g | Pro: 10g | Fat: 9g | Chol: 0mg | Sod: 300mg | Fiber: 5g | Sugars: 8g

13. Roasted Veggie Feast

Preparation time: 15 minutes
Servings: 4

Ingredients:

- 1 large zucchini, sliced
- 1 large red bell pepper, sliced
- 1 large yellow bell pepper, sliced
- 1 red onion, cut into wedges
- 1 cup cherry tomatoes
- 2 cloves garlic, minced
- 2 tbsp olive oil
- 1/2 tsp dried thyme
- 1/2 tsp dried rosemary
- 1/2 tsp dried oregano
- Salt and pepper to taste

Instructions:

1. Preheat your oven to 425°F (220°C).
2. In a large mixing bowl, combine the sliced zucchini, red and yellow bell peppers, red onion, cherry tomatoes, and minced garlic.
3. Drizzle the olive oil over the vegetables and toss them until evenly coated.
4. Sprinkle the dried thyme, rosemary, oregano, salt, and pepper over the vegetables and toss again to ensure even seasoning.
5. Spread the seasoned vegetables in a single layer on a large baking sheet.
6. Roast the vegetables in the preheated oven for 20-25 minutes or until they are tender and slightly caramelized, stirring halfway through the cooking time.
7. Once the vegetables are roasted to perfection, remove them from the oven.
8. Serve the Roasted Veggie Feast as a delicious and heart-healthy side dish or add it to salads, wraps, or grain bowls for a complete meal.

Nutritional Information (per serving):
Cal: 95 | Carbs: 9g | Pro: 2g | Fat: 6g | Chol: 0mg | Sod: 10mg | Fiber: 3g | Sugars: 5g

14. Pomegranate Kale Twist

Preparation time: 15 minutes
Servings: 2

Ingredients:

- 2 cups fresh kale leaves, chopped
- 1/2 cup pomegranate seeds
- 1/4 cup chopped walnuts
- 1/4 cup crumbled feta cheese
- 2 tbsp balsamic vinaigrette dressing (low sodium and low fat)

Instructions:

1. In a large mixing bowl, combine the chopped kale, pomegranate seeds, chopped walnuts, and crumbled feta cheese.
2. Drizzle the balsamic vinaigrette dressing over the ingredients in the bowl.
3. Toss the salad gently until all the ingredients are well coated with the dressing.
4. Divide the Pomegranate Kale Twist salad into two serving plates.
5. Serve immediately and enjoy!

Nutritional Information (per serving):
Cal: 180 | Carbs: 15g | Pro: 6g | Fat: 12g | Chol: 8mg | Sod: 140mg | Fiber: 3g | Sugars: 7g

15. Lemon Herb Shrimp Bowl

Preparation time: 15 minutes
Servings: 2

Ingredients:

- 1/2 lb (225g) medium shrimp, peeled and deveined
- 1 cup cooked quinoa or brown rice
- 1 cup fresh spinach leaves
- 1/2 cup cherry tomatoes, halved
- 1/4 cup red onion, thinly sliced
- 1/4 cup cucumber, diced
- 2 tbsp fresh parsley, chopped
- 2 tbsp fresh lemon juice
- 1 tbsp olive oil
- 1 clove garlic, minced
- 1/4 tsp dried oregano
- 1/4 tsp dried thyme
- Salt and pepper to taste

Instructions:

1. In a medium bowl, combine the shrimp, olive oil, minced garlic, dried oregano, dried thyme, salt, and pepper. Toss well to coat the shrimp evenly.
2. Heat a non-stick skillet over medium-high heat. Add the shrimp to the skillet and cook for 2-3 minutes per side until they turn pink and opaque. Remove from heat.
3. In a large bowl, assemble the shrimp bowl by layering cooked quinoa or brown rice, fresh spinach leaves, cherry tomatoes, red onion, and diced cucumber.
4. Add the cooked shrimp on top of the bed of vegetables and grains.
5. Drizzle fresh lemon juice over the bowl and sprinkle with chopped parsley.
6. Toss the ingredients together gently to combine all the flavors.
7. Serve the Lemon Herb Shrimp Bowl immediately while still warm.

Nutritional Information (per serving):
Cal: 280 | Carbs: 25g | Pro: 20g | Fat: 10g | Chol: 120mg | Sod: 300mg | Fiber: 4g | Sugars: 4g

16. Chickpea Tomato Tango

Preparation time: 15 minutes
Servings: 4

Ingredients:

- 1 can (15 oz) chickpeas, drained and rinsed
- 2 cups cherry tomatoes, halved
- 1 cucumber, diced
- 1/4 cup red onion, finely chopped
- 1/4 cup fresh parsley, chopped

- 2 tbsp extra-virgin olive oil
- 2 tbsp lemon juice
- 1 clove garlic, minced
- 1/4 tsp ground cumin
- Salt and pepper, to taste

Instructions:

1. In a large mixing bowl, combine the chickpeas, cherry tomatoes, cucumber, red onion, and fresh parsley.
2. In a small bowl, whisk together the olive oil, lemon juice, minced garlic, ground cumin, salt, and pepper.
3. Pour the dressing over the chickpea and tomato mixture, tossing gently to coat everything evenly.
4. Serve the Chickpea Tomato Tango salad immediately, or refrigerate for a few hours to let the flavors meld together.

Nutritional Information (per serving):
Cal: 220 | Carbs: 28g | Pro: 7g | Fat: 9g | Chol: 0mg | Sod: 350mg | Fiber: 8g | Sugars: 6g

17. Pear Walnut Serenade

Preparation time: 10 minutes
Servings: 2

Ingredients:

- 2 ripe pears, thinly sliced
- 1/4 cup chopped walnuts
- 1/4 tsp ground cinnamon
- 1 tsp honey (optional)

Instructions:

1. Arrange the thinly sliced pears on a serving platter.
2. Sprinkle the chopped walnuts over the pear slices.
3. Dust the pears and walnuts with ground cinnamon for added flavor.
4. Drizzle honey over the top if desired, for a touch of natural sweetness. (Note: If you're watching your sugar intake, you can skip the honey or use a small amount.)

Nutritional Information (per serving):
Cal: 120 | Carbs: 18g | Pro: 2g | Fat: 6g | Chol: 0mg | Sod: 0mg | Fiber: 5g | Sugars: 11g

18. Herbed Potato Harmony

Preparation time: 10 minutes
Servings: 4

Ingredients:

- 4 medium-sized potatoes, washed and diced

- 1 tbsp olive oil
- 1 tsp dried thyme
- 1 tsp dried rosemary
- 1/2 tsp garlic powder
- 1/2 tsp onion powder
- 1/4 tsp black pepper
- 1/4 tsp salt (optional)
- Fresh parsley, chopped, for garnish

Instructions:

1. Preheat your oven to 425°F (220°C).
2. In a large mixing bowl, combine the diced potatoes with olive oil, dried thyme, dried rosemary, garlic powder, onion powder, black pepper, and salt (if using). Toss the potatoes until evenly coated with the herbs and spices.
3. Line a baking sheet with parchment paper or lightly grease it with cooking spray. Spread the seasoned potatoes in a single layer on the baking sheet.
4. Place the baking sheet in the preheated oven and bake for about 20-25 minutes, or until the potatoes are tender and lightly browned, flipping them halfway through the cooking time for even browning.
5. Once the potatoes are cooked, remove them from the oven and transfer to a serving dish. Garnish with freshly chopped parsley.
6. Serve the Herbed Potato Harmony as a delicious and heart-healthy side dish with your favorite main course.

Nutritional Information (per serving):
Cal: 160 | Carbs: 28g | Pro: 3g | Fat: 4g | Chol: 0mg | Sod: 65mg | Fiber: 3g | Sugars: 2g

19. Orange Pecan Fantasy

Preparation time: 15 minutes
Servings: 4

Ingredients:

- 2 large oranges
- 1/4 cup chopped pecans
- 1 tbsp honey (optional, for added sweetness)
- 1/4 tsp ground cinnamon

Instructions:

1. Peel the oranges and remove any white pith. Separate the orange segments and place them in a large bowl.
2. In a dry skillet over medium heat, toast the chopped pecans for about 2-3 minutes, stirring frequently to avoid burning. Remove from heat and let them cool.
3. Sprinkle the toasted pecans over the orange segments.

4. If desired, drizzle honey over the oranges and pecans for added sweetness.
5. Sprinkle ground cinnamon on top for extra flavor.
6. Toss the mixture gently to combine all the ingredients.
7. Serve immediately or refrigerate for a refreshing chilled treat.

Nutritional Information (per serving):
Cal: 95 | Carbs: 16g | Pro: 1g | Fat: 4g | Chol: 0mg | Sod: 0mg | Fiber: 3g | Sugars: 12g

20. Ginger Carrot Crunch

Preparation time: 15 minutes
Servings: 4

Ingredients:

- 4 large carrots, peeled and julienned
- 1/4 cup unsalted almonds, chopped
- 1 tbsp fresh ginger, grated
- 2 tbsp rice vinegar
- 1 tbsp low-sodium soy sauce
- 1 tbsp honey
- 1 tsp sesame oil
- 1/4 tsp red pepper flakes (optional)
- 1 tbsp sesame seeds, for garnish

Instructions:

1. In a large bowl, combine the julienned carrots and chopped almonds.
2. In a separate small bowl, whisk together the grated ginger, rice vinegar, low-sodium soy sauce, honey, sesame oil, and red pepper flakes (if using).
3. Pour the dressing over the carrot and almond mixture. Toss well to combine, ensuring all the carrots are coated with the dressing.
4. Allow the Ginger Carrot Crunch to marinate for at least 5 minutes to let the flavors meld together.
5. Sprinkle sesame seeds on top for garnish before serving.

Nutritional Information (per serving):
Cal: 90 | Carbs: 12g | Pro: 3g | Fat: 4g | Chol: 0mg | Sod: 120mg | Fiber: 3g | Sugars: 7g

Desserts

1. Berry Chia Pudding Parfait

Preparation time: 10 minutes
Servings: 2

Ingredients:

- 1 cup unsweetened almond milk (or any preferred milk)
- 1/4 cup chia seeds
- 1 tsp honey or maple syrup (optional, for sweetness)
- 1/2 tsp vanilla extract
- 1 cup mixed berries (e.g., strawberries, blueberries, raspberries)

Instructions:

1. In a mixing bowl, combine the unsweetened almond milk, chia seeds, honey (if using), and vanilla extract. Stir well to ensure the chia seeds are evenly distributed. Let the mixture sit for 5 minutes.
2. After 5 minutes, give the mixture another stir to break up any clumps of chia seeds. Cover the bowl and refrigerate for at least 2 hours or preferably overnight to allow the chia seeds to absorb the liquid and create a pudding-like texture.
3. Once the chia pudding is ready and has thickened, give it a final stir to make sure it's smooth and creamy.
4. In serving glasses or parfait dishes, layer the chia pudding with the mixed berries. Start with a layer of chia pudding, followed by a layer of berries, and continue until all the ingredients are used up.
5. Top the berry chia pudding parfait with a few extra berries for garnish.
6. Serve immediately or refrigerate until ready to enjoy.

Nutritional Information (per serving):
Cal: 180 | Carbs: 23g | Pro: 6g | Fat: 7g | Chol: 0mg | Sod: 50mg | Fiber: 10g | Sugars: 9g

2. Citrus Angel Food Cake

Preparation time: 15 minutes
Servings: 8

Ingredients:

- 1 box (16 ounces) angel food cake mix
- 1 cup fresh orange juice
- 1 tbsp orange zest
- 1 tsp lemon zest
- 1/2 tsp vanilla extract
- 1/4 tsp salt

Instructions:

1. Preheat the oven to the temperature specified on the angel food cake mix package.
2. In a large mixing bowl, combine the angel food cake mix, fresh orange juice, orange zest, lemon zest, vanilla extract, and salt. Mix well until the batter is smooth and free of lumps.
3. Pour the batter into an ungreased angel food cake pan or a tube pan.
4. Bake the cake in the preheated oven for the time indicated on the cake mix package or until the top is golden brown and the cake springs back when touched.
5. Once the cake is done baking, remove it from the oven and immediately invert the pan onto a bottle or cooling rack to cool upside down. This helps prevent the cake from deflating.
6. Allow the cake to cool completely before removing it from the pan.
7. Serve the Citrus Angel Food Cake on its own or with a sprinkle of powdered sugar and fresh citrus slices for an extra burst of flavor.

Nutritional Information (per serving):
Cal: 160 | Carbs: 37g | Pro: 3g | Fat: 0.5g | Chol: 0mg | Sod: 270mg | Fiber: 0g | Sugars: 26g

3. Almond Flour Brownies

Preparation time: 15 minutes
Servings: 12

Ingredients:

- 1 cup almond flour
- 1/2 cup unsweetened cocoa powder
- 1/2 cup honey or maple syrup
- 1/4 cup unsweetened applesauce
- 2 large eggs
- 1/4 cup almond milk (or any milk of your choice)
- 1 tsp vanilla extract
- 1/2 tsp baking powder
- 1/4 tsp salt
- Cooking spray

Instructions:

1. Preheat your oven to 350°F (175°C). Grease an 8x8-inch baking pan with cooking spray and set aside.
2. In a large mixing bowl, whisk together the almond flour, cocoa powder, baking powder, and salt.
3. In a separate bowl, whisk together the honey (or maple syrup), unsweetened applesauce, eggs, almond milk, and vanilla extract until well combined.
4. Add the wet ingredients to the dry ingredients and stir until you have a smooth batter.
5. Pour the batter into the prepared baking pan, spreading it evenly.
6. Bake in the preheated oven for 20-25 minutes or until a toothpick inserted into the center comes out with a few moist crumbs (be careful not to

overbake).

7. Remove the brownies from the oven and let them cool completely in the pan on a wire rack.
8. Once cooled, cut the brownies into 12 squares and serve.

Nutritional Information (per serving):
Cal: 120 | Carbs: 14g | Pro: 3g | Fat: 7g | Chol: 31mg | Sod: 60mg | Fiber: 2g | Sugars: 9g

4. Mango Sorbet Delight

Preparation time: 10 minutes
Servings: 4

Ingredients:

- 3 ripe mangoes, peeled and diced
- 1/4 cup water
- 2 tbsp honey (or preferred sweetener)
- 1 tsp lime juice
- Fresh mint leaves (optional, for garnish)

Instructions:

1. In a blender or food processor, add the diced mangoes, water, honey, and lime juice.
2. Blend the ingredients until you get a smooth and creamy mixture.
3. Taste the mixture and adjust the sweetness by adding more honey if needed.
4. Pour the mango mixture into a shallow, freezer-safe container.
5. Cover the container and place it in the freezer for at least 4 hours or until the sorbet is firm.
6. Once the sorbet is frozen, scoop it into serving bowls or glasses.
7. Garnish with fresh mint leaves, if desired.
8. Serve immediately and enjoy the refreshing and heart-healthy Mango Sorbet Delight!

Nutritional Information (per serving):
Cal: 100 | Carbs: 25g | Pro: 1g | Fat: 0.5g | Chol: 0mg | Sod: 0mg | Fiber: 2g | Sugars: 22g

5. Apple Cinnamon Crumble Bars

Preparation time: 15 minutes
Servings: 12 bars

Ingredients:

- 1 cup old-fashioned oats
- 1 cup whole wheat flour
- 1/2 cup unsweetened applesauce
- 1/4 cup honey or maple syrup
- 1/4 cup coconut oil, melted
- 1/2 tsp baking soda
- 1/4 tsp salt

- 1 tsp ground cinnamon

For the apple filling:

- 3 cups apples, peeled and diced (about 3 medium apples)
- 1 tbsp lemon juice
- 2 tbsp honey or maple syrup
- 1/2 tsp ground cinnamon
- 1/4 tsp ground nutmeg

Instructions:

1. Preheat your oven to 350°F (175°C). Grease an 8x8-inch baking dish with cooking spray or line it with parchment paper for easy removal.
2. In a large mixing bowl, combine the oats, whole wheat flour, baking soda, salt, and 1 tsp ground cinnamon. Stir until well combined.
3. In a separate bowl, mix the unsweetened applesauce, honey or maple syrup, and melted coconut oil.
4. Pour the wet ingredients into the dry ingredients and mix until everything is well combined, forming a crumbly mixture.
5. Set aside about 3/4 cup of the mixture to use as the crumble topping later.
6. Press the rest of the mixture firmly into the bottom of the prepared baking dish to form the crust.
7. In another bowl, toss the diced apples with lemon juice, honey or maple syrup, 1/2 tsp ground cinnamon, and ground nutmeg until the apples are coated.
8. Spread the apple filling evenly over the crust in the baking dish.
9. Sprinkle the reserved crumble mixture on top of the apple filling.
10. Bake in the preheated oven for about 30 minutes or until the crumble topping turns golden brown.
11. Remove from the oven and let it cool completely in the baking dish before cutting it into 12 bars.

Nutritional Information (per serving):
Cal: 180 | Carbs: 26g | Pro: 2g | Fat: 8g | Chol: 0mg | Sod: 40mg | Fiber: 3g | Sugars: 13g

6. Dark Chocolate Dipped Strawberries

Preparation time: 15 minutes
Servings: 4

Ingredients:

- 1 cup dark chocolate chips (look for low-fat and low-sodium options)
- 1 pound fresh strawberries, washed and dried

Instructions:

1. Line a baking sheet with parchment paper.

2. In a microwave-safe bowl, melt the dark chocolate chips in the microwave in 30-second intervals, stirring between each interval, until the chocolate is smooth and fully melted.
3. Hold each strawberry by the stem and dip it into the melted chocolate, swirling it to coat about two-thirds of the strawberry with chocolate.
4. Place the chocolate-dipped strawberries on the prepared baking sheet.
5. Once all strawberries are dipped, refrigerate the baking sheet for about 10 minutes to allow the chocolate to set.
6. Once the chocolate is set, the Dark Chocolate Dipped Strawberries are ready to be served.

Nutritional Information (per serving):
Cal: 150 | Carbs: 25g | Pro: 2g | Fat: 8g | Chol: 0mg | Sod: 0mg | Fiber: 4g | Sugars: 18g

7. Lemon Poppy Seed Muffins

Preparation time: 15 minutes
Servings: 12 muffins

Ingredients:

- 1 1/2 cups whole wheat flour
- 1/2 cup all-purpose flour
- 1/3 cup granulated sugar
- 1/4 cup honey
- 2 tbsp poppy seeds
- 1 tbsp baking powder
- 1/2 tsp baking soda
- 1/4 tsp salt
- 1 cup low-fat plain yogurt
- 1/4 cup unsweetened applesauce
- 1/4 cup fresh lemon juice
- 1 tbsp lemon zest
- 1 tsp vanilla extract
- 2 large eggs

Instructions:

1. Preheat your oven to 375°F (190°C). Line a muffin tin with paper liners or lightly grease each cup.
2. In a large mixing bowl, combine the whole wheat flour, all-purpose flour, sugar, poppy seeds, baking powder, baking soda, and salt.
3. In a separate bowl, whisk together the yogurt, applesauce, honey, lemon juice, lemon zest, vanilla extract, and eggs until well combined.
4. Pour the wet ingredients into the dry ingredients and gently stir until just combined. Do not overmix; the batter should be slightly lumpy.
5. Divide the batter evenly among the prepared muffin cups, filling each about two-thirds full.
6. Bake the muffins in the preheated oven for 15-18 minutes or until a toothpick inserted into the center of a muffin comes out clean.
7. Remove the muffins from the oven and let them

cool in the muffin tin for 5 minutes before transferring them to a wire rack to cool completely.

Nutritional Information (per serving):
Cal: 157 | Carbs: 29g | Pro: 4g | Fat: 3g | Chol: 32mg | Sod: 198mg | Fiber: 2g | Sugars: 11g

8. Baked Peaches with Honey

Preparation time: 10 minutes
Servings: 4

Ingredients:

- 4 ripe peaches, halved and pitted
- 2 tablespoons honey
- 1/4 teaspoon ground cinnamon
- 1/4 teaspoon vanilla extract
- Cooking spray

Instructions:

1. Preheat your oven to 375°F (190°C).
2. Line a baking sheet with parchment paper and lightly coat it with cooking spray.
3. Place the peach halves on the prepared baking sheet, cut side up.
4. In a small bowl, mix together the honey, ground cinnamon, and vanilla extract.
5. Drizzle the honey mixture evenly over the peach halves.
6. Bake the peaches in the preheated oven for about 15-20 minutes or until they are tender and slightly caramelized.
7. Remove the baked peaches from the oven and let them cool for a few minutes before serving.
8. Optionally, you can serve the baked peaches with a dollop of Greek yogurt or a sprinkle of chopped nuts for added texture and flavor.

Nutritional Information (per serving):
Cal: 74 | Carbs: 18g | Pro: 1g | Fat: 0g | Chol: 0mg | Sod: 0mg | Fiber: 2g | Sugars: 16g

9. Vanilla Yogurt Fruit Cups

Preparation time: 10 minutes
Servings: 2

Ingredients:

- 1 cup low-fat vanilla yogurt
- 1 cup mixed fresh fruits (e.g., berries, diced melon, sliced kiwi)
- 1 tablespoon honey (optional, for added sweetness)

Instructions:

1. In a bowl, combine the low-fat vanilla yogurt with

honey (if using) and mix well.
2. Wash and prepare the mixed fresh fruits, cutting them into bite-sized pieces as needed.
3. In serving cups or small bowls, layer the vanilla yogurt and mixed fruits alternately, creating colorful and appealing fruit cups.
4. Repeat the layers until the cups are filled to your desired level, finishing with a layer of fruits on top.
5. Serve the Vanilla Yogurt Fruit Cups immediately, or cover and refrigerate for a refreshing treat later.

Nutritional Information (per serving):
Cal: 120 | Carbs: 24g | Pro: 5g | Fat: 1g | Chol: 5mg | Sod: 50mg | Fiber: 2g | Sugars: 20g

10. Raspberry Oatmeal Cookies

Preparation time: 15 minutes
Servings: 12 cookies

Ingredients:

- 1 cup rolled oats
- 1/2 cup whole wheat flour
- 1/4 cup unsweetened applesauce
- 2 tablespoons honey
- 1/4 cup fresh raspberries, mashed
- 1/4 teaspoon baking soda
- 1/4 teaspoon ground cinnamon
- 1/4 teaspoon vanilla extract

Instructions:

1. Preheat the oven to 350°F (175°C). Line a baking sheet with parchment paper or use a non-stick baking mat.
2. In a mixing bowl, combine the rolled oats, whole wheat flour, baking soda, and ground cinnamon.
3. In a separate bowl, mix the unsweetened applesauce, honey, and vanilla extract until well combined.
4. Add the wet ingredients to the dry ingredients and stir until a dough forms.
5. Gently fold in the mashed raspberries into the cookie dough.
6. Take spoonfuls of the dough and drop them onto the prepared baking sheet, spacing them apart.
7. Flatten each cookie slightly with the back of the spoon.
8. Bake the cookies in the preheated oven for 12-15 minutes or until the edges turn golden brown.
9. Remove from the oven and let the cookies cool on the baking sheet for a few minutes before transferring them to a wire rack to cool completely.

Nutritional Information (per serving):
Cal: 80 | Carbs: 14g | Pro: 2g | Fat: 1g | Chol: 0mg | Sod: 22mg | Fiber: 2g | Sugars: 5g

11. Pineapple Mint Frozen Treats

Preparation time: 10 minutes
Servings: 4

Ingredients:

- 2 cups frozen pineapple chunks
- 1/4 cup fresh mint leaves
- 1/2 cup plain low-fat Greek yogurt
- 1 tbsp honey (optional, for added sweetness)
- 1/2 tsp vanilla extract

Instructions:

1. In a blender or food processor, combine the frozen pineapple chunks, fresh mint leaves, Greek yogurt, honey (if using), and vanilla extract.
2. Blend the ingredients until smooth and creamy, scraping down the sides of the blender or food processor as needed.
3. Taste the mixture and adjust sweetness to your liking by adding more honey if desired.
4. Pour the pineapple mint mixture into popsicle molds or a shallow dish.
5. If using popsicle molds, insert popsicle sticks into each mold.
6. Place the molds or dish in the freezer and freeze for at least 4 hours or until the treats are completely frozen.
7. Once frozen, remove the treats from the molds or cut them into desired shapes if using a dish.
8. Serve the Pineapple Mint Frozen Treats immediately or store them in an airtight container in the freezer for up to 2 weeks.

Nutritional Information (per serving):
Cal: 75 | Carbs: 17g | Pro: 2g | Fat: 0g | Chol: 0mg | Sod: 9mg | Fiber: 1g | Sugars: 13g

12. Carrot Cake Bites

Preparation time: 15 minutes
Servings: 12

Ingredients:

- 1 cup grated carrots
- 1/2 cup rolled oats
- 1/2 cup unsweetened shredded coconut
- 1/4 cup chopped walnuts
- 1/4 cup raisins
- 2 tablespoons honey
- 1/2 teaspoon ground cinnamon
- 1/4 teaspoon ground nutmeg
- 1/4 teaspoon vanilla extract
- Pinch of salt

Instructions:

1. In a large mixing bowl, combine the grated carrots, rolled oats, shredded coconut, chopped walnuts, and raisins.
2. In a small microwave-safe bowl, warm the honey for a few seconds until it becomes more liquid.
3. Pour the warm honey over the dry ingredients in the large bowl.
4. Add the ground cinnamon, ground nutmeg, vanilla extract, and a pinch of salt to the mixture.
5. Mix all the ingredients thoroughly until well combined.
6. Place the mixture in the refrigerator for about 10 minutes. Chilling will make it easier to form the carrot cake bites.
7. Once the mixture is chilled, take small portions and roll them into bite-sized balls using your hands.
8. Place the carrot cake bites on a plate or tray lined with parchment paper.
9. Store the carrot cake bites in an airtight container in the refrigerator for up to a week.

Nutritional Information (per serving):
Cal: 80 | Carbs: 10g | Pro: 1g | Fat: 4g | Chol: 0mg | Sod: 10mg | Fiber: 1g | Sugars: 6g

13. Pistachio Date Energy Balls

Preparation time: 15 minutes
Servings: 12 balls

Ingredients:

- 1 cup pitted dates
- 1 cup raw unsalted pistachios
- 2 tablespoons unsweetened shredded coconut
- 1 tablespoon chia seeds
- 1/2 teaspoon pure vanilla extract
- 1/4 teaspoon ground cinnamon
- Pinch of salt

Instructions:

1. In a food processor, add the pitted dates, pistachios, shredded coconut, chia seeds, vanilla extract, ground cinnamon, and a pinch of salt.
2. Pulse the ingredients until they are well combined and the mixture starts to form a sticky dough.
3. Take a small amount of the mixture and roll it between your palms to form a ball, about the size of a walnut.
4. Repeat the process with the rest of the mixture, making approximately 12 energy balls.
5. Place the energy balls on a plate and refrigerate them for at least 30 minutes to firm up.
6. Once chilled, transfer the energy balls to an airtight container and store them in the refrigerator.

Nutritional Information (per serving):
Cal: 115 | Carbs: 15g | Pro: 2g | Fat: 6g | Chol: 0mg | Sod: 0mg | Fiber: 3g | Sugars: 10g

14. Blueberry Oat Crisp

Preparation time: 15 minutes
Servings: 6

Ingredients:

- 4 cups fresh blueberries
- 1 tablespoon lemon juice
- 1/4 cup honey or maple syrup
- 1/2 cup rolled oats
- 1/4 cup whole wheat flour
- 2 tablespoons almond flour
- 2 tablespoons chopped almonds
- 1/4 teaspoon ground cinnamon
- 2 tablespoons coconut oil, melted
- Cooking spray

Instructions:

1. Preheat the oven to 350°F (175°C). Lightly grease a baking dish with cooking spray.
2. In a large bowl, toss the blueberries with lemon juice and honey or maple syrup until well coated. Transfer the blueberries to the greased baking dish, spreading them out evenly.
3. In the same bowl, combine rolled oats, whole wheat flour, almond flour, chopped almonds, and ground cinnamon. Mix well.
4. Pour the melted coconut oil over the dry ingredients and stir until the mixture becomes crumbly.
5. Sprinkle the oat mixture evenly over the blueberries in the baking dish.
6. Bake in the preheated oven for 25-30 minutes or until the blueberries are bubbling, and the topping turns golden brown.
7. Remove from the oven and let it cool for a few minutes before serving.

Nutritional Information (per serving):
Cal: 200 | Carbs: 34g | Pro: 3g | Fat: 7g | Chol: 0mg | Sod: 2mg | Fiber: 5g | Sugars: 21g

15. Kiwi Lime Sorbet Cups

Preparation time: 10 minutes
Servings: 4

Ingredients:

- 4 ripe kiwis, peeled and diced
- Juice of 2 limes
- 2 tbsp honey (or any preferred sweetener)
- 1/4 cup water
- Lime zest (optional, for garnish)

Instructions:

1. In a blender or food processor, combine the diced kiwis, lime juice, honey, and water.

2. Blend the mixture until smooth and well combined. If needed, add more water to achieve the desired consistency.
3. Taste the sorbet mixture and adjust the sweetness by adding more honey if desired.
4. Pour the sorbet mixture into a shallow container or ice cube tray and freeze for at least 4 hours or until solid.
5. Once the sorbet is frozen, remove it from the container and let it sit at room temperature for a few minutes to soften slightly.
6. To serve, scoop the kiwi lime sorbet into small cups or bowls.
7. Garnish with lime zest if desired.

Nutritional Information (per serving):
Cal: 60 | Carbs: 15g | Pro: 1g | Fat: 0g | Chol: 0mg | Sod: 2mg | Fiber: 2g | Sugars: 10g

16. Banana Walnut Bites

Preparation time: 10 minutes
Servings: 12

Ingredients:

- 2 ripe bananas, mashed
- 1 cup old-fashioned oats
- 1/4 cup chopped walnuts
- 1/4 cup unsweetened applesauce
- 1 tsp vanilla extract
- 1/2 tsp ground cinnamon
- Cooking spray

Instructions:

1. Preheat your oven to 350°F (175°C) and lightly grease a baking sheet with cooking spray.
2. In a mixing bowl, combine the mashed bananas, oats, chopped walnuts, unsweetened applesauce, vanilla extract, and ground cinnamon. Stir well until all the ingredients are thoroughly combined.
3. Scoop small spoonfuls of the mixture and drop them onto the greased baking sheet, forming bite-sized rounds. Flatten the rounds slightly with the back of the spoon.
4. Bake the banana walnut bites in the preheated oven for about 12-15 minutes or until they become golden brown.
5. Remove the bites from the oven and let them cool on the baking sheet for a few minutes before transferring them to a wire rack to cool completely.
6. Once cooled, the Banana Walnut Bites are ready to be served. Enjoy these heart-healthy and delicious treats!

Nutritional Information (per serving):
Cal: 67 | Carbs: 10g | Pro: 1g | Fat: 3g | Chol: 0mg | Sod: 0mg | Fiber: 1g | Sugars: 3g

17. Cinnamon Baked Apples

Preparation time: 10 minutes
Servings: 4

Ingredients:

- 4 large apples (such as Granny Smith or Honeycrisp)
- 1 tablespoon lemon juice
- 1 tablespoon honey
- 1 teaspoon ground cinnamon
- 1/4 teaspoon ground nutmeg
- Cooking spray

Instructions:

1. Preheat the oven to 375°F (190°C).
2. Wash the apples thoroughly and core them, removing the seeds and stem. Leave the skin on for added nutrition and texture.
3. In a small bowl, mix the lemon juice, honey, ground cinnamon, and ground nutmeg until well combined.
4. Place the cored apples in a baking dish and spoon the cinnamon-honey mixture into each apple's center.
5. Lightly spray the apples with cooking spray to prevent sticking and add a touch of moisture.
6. Bake the apples in the preheated oven for 25-30 minutes or until they become tender. You can test the doneness by piercing the apples with a fork.
7. Once baked, remove the apples from the oven and let them cool for a few minutes before serving.
8. Optionally, serve the cinnamon baked apples with a dollop of low-fat Greek yogurt or a sprinkle of chopped nuts for extra heart-healthy goodness.

Nutritional Information (per serving):
Cal: 116 | Carbs: 30g | Pro: 0.5g | Fat: 0.2g | Chol: 0mg | Sod: 1mg | Fiber: 5g | Sugars: 23g

18. Cranberry Orange Biscotti

Preparation time: 15 minutes
Servings: 12

Ingredients:

- 1 3/4 cups all-purpose flour
- 1/2 cup granulated sugar
- 1/2 tsp baking powder
- 1/4 tsp salt
- 2 large eggs
- 2 tbsp orange juice
- 1 tsp vanilla extract
- 1/2 cup dried cranberries
- Zest of 1 orange

Instructions:

1. Preheat your oven to 350°F (175°C) and line a baking sheet with parchment paper.
2. In a large mixing bowl, whisk together the flour, sugar, baking powder, and salt.
3. In a separate bowl, beat the eggs with the orange juice and vanilla extract.
4. Gradually add the wet ingredients to the dry ingredients, stirring until a dough forms.
5. Fold in the dried cranberries and orange zest until evenly distributed.
6. On a lightly floured surface, shape the dough into a log about 12 inches long and 3 inches wide.
7. Place the log onto the prepared baking sheet and flatten it slightly.
8. Bake the biscotti log for 25 minutes or until firm to the touch.
9. Remove the log from the oven and let it cool for 10 minutes.
10. Reduce the oven temperature to 325°F (160°C).
11. Using a sharp knife, slice the log diagonally into 12 even pieces.
12. Place the biscotti slices back on the baking sheet, cut side up, and bake for an additional 10 minutes.
13. Flip the biscotti over and bake for another 10 minutes or until they are crisp and golden.
14. Let the biscotti cool completely on a wire rack before serving.

Nutritional Information (per serving):
Cal: 120 | Carbs: 23g | Pro: 2g | Fat: 2g | Chol: 28mg | Sod: 75mg | Fiber: 1g | Sugars: 10g

19. Coconut Lime Rice Pudding

Preparation time: 5 minutes
Servings: 4

Ingredients:

- 1 cup cooked white rice
- 1 can (13.5 oz) light coconut milk
- 1/4 cup low-fat milk (or plant-based milk for vegan option)
- 2 tbsp honey or maple syrup
- Zest of 1 lime
- 1/4 tsp vanilla extract
- Pinch of salt
- Lime wedges and toasted coconut flakes for garnish (optional)

Instructions:

1. In a medium saucepan, combine the cooked white rice, light coconut milk, and low-fat milk. Stir well to combine.
2. Place the saucepan over medium heat and bring the mixture to a simmer. Stir occasionally to prevent sticking.

3. Add honey or maple syrup, lime zest, vanilla extract, and a pinch of salt to the rice mixture. Stir to incorporate all the flavors.
4. Let the rice pudding simmer for about 5-7 minutes or until it reaches your desired consistency. If it thickens too much, you can add a little more milk to adjust.
5. Once the rice pudding is creamy and cooked to your liking, remove the saucepan from the heat.
6. Serve the Coconut Lime Rice Pudding warm in individual bowls. Garnish with lime wedges and toasted coconut flakes, if desired.

Nutritional Information (per serving):
Cal: 230 | Carbs: 39g | Pro: 3g | Fat: 7g | Chol: 0mg | Sod: 30mg | Fiber: 1g | Sugars: 14g

20. Mixed Berry Parfait

Preparation time: 10 minutes
Servings: 2

Ingredients:

- 1 cup non-fat Greek yogurt
- 1 cup mixed berries (strawberries, blueberries, raspberries)
- 1 tablespoon honey or maple syrup (optional)
- 1/4 cup low-fat granola (low-sodium)

Instructions:

1. Wash the mixed berries thoroughly and pat them dry with a paper towel.
2. In a bowl, mix the non-fat Greek yogurt with honey or maple syrup (if using), ensuring it's well combined. Set aside.
3. Take two serving glasses or bowls and start assembling the parfaits.
4. Begin by layering a spoonful of the yogurt mixture at the bottom of each glass.
5. Add a layer of mixed berries on top of the yogurt.
6. Sprinkle a tablespoon of the low-fat granola over the berries.
7. Repeat the layers until the glasses are filled, finishing with a layer of berries and a sprinkle of granola on top.
8. Refrigerate the parfaits for about 30 minutes before serving. This allows the flavors to meld together and the parfait to slightly set.

Nutritional Information (per serving):
Cal: 160 | Carbs: 31g | Pro: 12g | Fat: 1g | Chol: 4mg | Sod: 32mg | Fiber: 4g | Sugars: 21g

Meal Plan

DAY	BREAKFAST	LUNCH	DINNER
1	Veggie Egg Muffins	Citrus Avocado Delight	Herb-Roasted Chicken Delight
2	Avocado Toast Delight	Lemon-Garlic Grilled Turkey Breast	Zesty Citrus Salmon Bake
3	Chia Berry Parfait	Ginger-Lime Glazed Chicken Skewers	Baked Dijon Cod Fillets
4	Quinoa Fruit Bowl	Balsamic-Basil Stuffed Chicken	Grilled Garlic Prawns
5	Almond Banana Smoothie	Dijon Mustard Turkey Tenderloins	Cajun Blackened Catfish
6	Spinach Omelet Roll	Paprika-Rubbed Roast Chicken Thighs	Mediterranean Stuffed Squid
7	Greek Yogurt Crunch	Rosemary-Lemon Grilled Chicken Legs	Lime Cilantro Mahi-Mahi
8	Apple Cinnamon Pancakes	Apricot-Glazed Baked Turkey Meatballs	Poached Halibut in Broth
9	Oats & Berries Bowl	Tandoori Chicken Lettuce Wraps	Lemon Pepper Trout Fillets
10	Sweet Potato Hash Browns	Pesto-Marinated Grilled Turkey Cutlets	Coconut Curry Shrimp Stir-fry
11	Pesto Egg Wraps	Cilantro-Lime Chicken and Rice	Balsamic Roasted Brussels Sprouts
12	Blueberry Flaxseed Muffins	Garlic-Herb Roasted Turkey Wings	Herbed Brown Rice Pilaf
13	Tofu Scramble Fiesta	Orange-Rosemary Baked Chicken Quarters	Zucchini Noodles Primavera
14	Coconut Chia Pudding	Mediterranean Stuffed Turkey Zucchini Boats	Chickpea Avocado Salad
15	Raspberry Almond Bites	Honey-Mustard Glazed Chicken Tenders	Turmeric Spiced Couscous
16	Mushroom Spinach Frittata	Teriyaki Pineapple Turkey Skillet	Ratatouille Stuffed Eggplant
17	Pear Walnut Oatmeal	Italian Herb Roasted Chicken Legs	Cilantro Lime Brown Rice
18	Breakfast Stuffed Peppers	Lemon-Pepper Turkey Breast Slices	Caprese Quinoa Skewers
19	Cranberry Orange Scones	Moroccan Spiced Chicken Stir-Fry	Asparagus Lemon Risotto
20	Tomato Basil Feta Salad	Buffalo Chicken Cauliflower Bites	Sweet Potato Kale Hash
21	Zesty Avocado Salad Cups	Steamed Ginger Soy Snapper	Quinoa Spinach Stuffed Tomatoes
22	Quinoa Stuffed Peppers	Spicy Black Bean Chili	Roasted Garlic Cauliflower Mash
23	Lemon-Herb Baked Cauliflower	Cabbage Tomato Detox Soup	Citrus Avocado Delight
24	Cucumber Tomato Bites	Creamy Avocado Lime Gazpacho	Spinach Berry Medley
25	Roasted Garlic Hummus Dip	Moroccan Chickpea Stew	Quinoa Veggie Mix
26	Spinach Mushroom Sauté	Lemon Herb Quinoa Salad	Mediterranean Power Bowl
27	Greek Yogurt Veggie Dip	Lime Cilantro Quinoa	Zesty Tuna Crunch
28	Balsamic Bruschetta Toast	Broccoli Almond Crunch	Cucumber Dill Bliss
29	Steamed Asparagus Spears	Sweet Potato Chickpea Salad	Beetroot Apple Slaw

DAY	BREAKFAST	LUNCH	DINNER
30	Herbed Chickpea Salad	Turmeric Spiced Roasted Cauliflower	Grilled Peach Arugula
31	Greek Yogurt Veggie Dip	Lemon Herb Quinoa Salad	Lemon-Garlic Grilled Turkey Breast
32	Balsamic Bruschetta Toast	Chickpea Avocado Salad	Zesty Citrus Salmon Bake
33	Steamed Asparagus Spears	Mediterranean Power Bowl	Seared Tuna Steaks with Salsa
34	Herbed Chickpea Salad	Quinoa Veggie Mix	Baked Dijon Cod Fillets
35	Roasted Garlic Hummus Dip	Lime Cilantro Quinoa	Poached Halibut in Broth
36	Spinach Mushroom Sauté	Sweet Potato Chickpea Salad	Grilled Garlic Prawns
37	Greek Yogurt Crunch	Turmeric Spiced Roasted Cauliflower	Coconut Curry Shrimp Stir-fry
38	Apple Cinnamon Pancakes	Ratatouille Stuffed Eggplant	Cajun Blackened Catfish
39	Oats & Berries Bowl	Caprese Quinoa Skewers	Mediterranean Stuffed Squid
40	Sweet Potato Hash Browns	Asparagus Lemon Risotto	Lime Cilantro Mahi-Mahi
41	Pesto Egg Wraps	Roasted Garlic Cauliflower Mash	Balsamic Roasted Brussels Sprouts
42	Blueberry Flaxseed Muffins	Citrus Avocado Delight	Lemon Pepper Trout Fillets
43	Tofu Scramble Fiesta	Spinach Berry Medley	Zesty Tuna Crunch
44	Coconut Chia Pudding	Quinoa Veggie Mix	Grilled Peach Arugula
45	Raspberry Almond Bites	Beetroot Apple Slaw	Zesty Citrus Salmon Bake
46	Mushroom Spinach Frittata	Cucumber Dill Bliss	Seared Tuna Steaks with Salsa
47	Pear Walnut Oatmeal	Broccoli Almond Crunch	Baked Dijon Cod Fillets
48	Breakfast Stuffed Peppers	Sweet Potato Chickpea Salad	Poached Halibut in Broth
49	Cranberry Orange Scones	Mediterranean Power Bowl	Grilled Garlic Prawns
50	Tomato Basil Feta Salad	Lime Cilantro Quinoa	Coconut Curry Shrimp Stir-fry
51	Zesty Avocado Salad Cups	Ratatouille Stuffed Eggplant	Cajun Blackened Catfish
52	Quinoa Stuffed Peppers	Caprese Quinoa Skewers	Mediterranean Stuffed Squid
53	Lemon-Herb Baked Cauliflower	Asparagus Lemon Risotto	Lime Cilantro Mahi-Mahi
54	Cucumber Tomato Bites	Roasted Garlic Cauliflower Mash	Balsamic Roasted Brussels Sprouts
55	Roasted Garlic Hummus Dip	Citrus Avocado Delight	Lemon Pepper Trout Fillets
56	Spinach Mushroom Sauté	Spinach Berry Medley	Zesty Tuna Crunch
57	Greek Yogurt Veggie Dip	Quinoa Veggie Mix	Grilled Peach Arugula
58	Balsamic Bruschetta Toast	Beetroot Apple Slaw	Zesty Citrus Salmon Bake
59	Steamed Asparagus Spears	Broccoli Almond Crunch	Seared Tuna Steaks with Salsa
60	Herbed Chickpea Salad	Sweet Potato Chickpea Salad	Baked Dijon Cod Fillets

Conversion Tables

VOLUME EQUIVALENTS (DRY)

US STANDARD	METRIC (APPROXIMATE)
1/8 Teaspoon	0.5 ml
1/4 Teaspoon	1 ml
1/2 Teaspoon	2 ml
3/4 Teaspoon	4 ml
1 Teaspoon	5 ml
1 Tablespoon	15 ml
1/4 Cup	59 ml
1/2 Cup	118 ml
3/4 Cup	177 ml
1 Cup	235 ml
2 Cups	475 ml
3 Cups	700 ml
4 Cups	1 l

WEIGHT EQUIVALENTS

US STANDARD	METRIC (APPROXIMATE)
1 Ounce	28 g
2 Ounces	57 g
5 Ounces	142 g
10 Ounces	284 g
15 Ounces	425 g
16 Ounces (1 Pound)	455g
1.5 Pounds	680 g
2 Pounds	907 g

TEMPERATURES EQUIVALENTS

FAHRENHEIT (F)	CELSIUS (C) (APPROXIMATE)
225 °F	107 °C
250 °F	120 °C
275 °F	135 °C
300 °F	150 °C
325 °F	160 °C
350 °F	180 °C
375 °F	190 °C
400 °F	205 °C
425 °F	220 °C
450 °F	235 °C
475 °F	245 °C
500 °F	260 °C

VOLUME EQUIVALENTS (LIQUID)

US STANDARD	US STANDARD (OUNCES)	METRIC (APPROXIMATE)
2 Tablespoons	1 fl.oz.	30 ml
1/4 Cup	2 fl.oz.	60 ml
1/2 Cup	4 fl.oz.	120 ml
1 Cup	8 fl.oz.	240 ml
1 1/2 Cups	12 fl.oz.	355 ml
2 Cups or 1 Pint	16 fl.oz.	475 ml
4 Cups or 1 Quart	32 fl.oz.	1 l
1 Gallon	128 fl.oz.	4 l

Bonus

Would you like to download my cookbook with 50 recipes for diabetes now?

It's easy!

Scan this QR Code and follow all the directions!

If there are problems and you can't download the recipes, email me at
bonus.violetharmond@gmail.com and I'll be happy to help!

Printed in Great Britain
by Amazon

46344346R00053